CONCILIUM
Religion in the Seventies

CONCILIUM

Concilium 1, 1977: Sociology of Religion

ETHNICITY

Edited by

Andrew M. Greeley
and Gregory Baum

seminary library

Charles L. Souvay Memorial

A CROSSROAD BOOK
The Seabury Press • New York

1977
The Seabury Press
815 Second Avenue
New York, N.Y. 10017

Library of Congress Catalog Card Number: 76-57796
ISBN: 0-8164-2145-5
Printed in the United States of America

Contents

PART I

Social Observations

Walker and Mary Connor

Political Fusion and
Ethnic Fission in Western Europe

DURING the past decade, ethnonational movements within Western Europe have become too numerous to be explained away on a case by case basis as either unique or vestigial. Some of the situations have demanded great publicity. Thus, the large-scale restiveness among Spain's Basque and Catalan communities has been well publicized. So too has the revitalization of the Scottish and Welsh nationalist movements within the United Kingdom, as well as the attritional struggle being waged in Northern Ireland between those of Irish and non-Irish descent (a struggle commonly but erroneously described as Catholic versus Protestant). The threat posed to the survival of Belgium by the intense rivalry between Flemings and Walloons has necessarily received great attention. And the French government was compelled to publicly acknowledge substantial internal unrest in January 1974, when it outlawed extant national liberation movements among the Bretons, (French) Basques, and Corsicans. Still other well publicized cases of ethnically inspired unrest have been associated with the German-speaking element of Alpine Italy and the French-speaking element of Bern Canton in Switzerland.

Less well advertised illustrations of growing self-assertiveness on the part of ethnonational groups also abound. A secret meeting of the representatives of such groups, which was held at Trieste in July 1974, was reported to have been attended by delegates of, *inter alia*, the Alsatians (France), the Frisians (the Netherlands), the Galicians (Spain), the Occitanians (France), the Piedmontese (Italy), and the Sardinians. More recently, a Celtic League Conference included delegates from "Kernow" and "Manin" (i.e., Cornwall and the Isle of Man). Still other groups which have offered some sign of ethnically inspired, post-war restiveness might include the Croats and

1

Slovenes of Austria; the Norse-descended inhabitants of the Danish-controlled Faroe Islands, as well as the Eskimo population of Danish-controlled Greenland; and the Calabrians, Sicilians, Slovenes, and Val d'Aostans of Italy.

Rare indeed is the individual who can claim to have anticipated this surge of ethnonationalism. Throughout the preceding century, some of the world's most influential publicists had given assurances that political loyalties were not an issue within one or another of the presently affected states. Thus, in 1861, John Stuart Mill wrote in *Considerations on Representative Government* that the matter of political identity appeared settled in the cases of Belgium and Switzerland. The following year, in an article entitled "Nationality," Lord Acton would say of the ethnically diverse peoples of Switzerland, "No nationality has the slightest claim upon them, except the purely political nationality of Switzerland." In 1866, Friedrich Engels in "What Have the Working Class to Do with Poland?" would maintain that "the Highland Gaels and the Welsh are undoubtedly of different nationalities to what the English are, although nobody will give to these remnants of people long gone by the title of nations, any more than to the Celtic inhabitants of Brittany in France." Shortly after World War I, Sir Ernest Barker (*National Character and the Factors in Its Formation*) would describe the United Kingdom and Switzerland as states in which the matter of political loyalties was settled. During World War II, Alfred Cobban (*National Self-Determination*) would agree, adding Belgium wherein he could detect "no reason at all" to feel that ethnic identities challenged the state structure.

Things did not change significantly in the postwar era. Karl Deutsch, probably the most prominent contemporary scholar of nationalism, published his *Nationalism and Social Communication* in 1953, within which he employed Bretons, Flemings, Franco- and German-Swiss, Scots, and Welsh as examples of completely assimilated peoples. And in a 1969 work by the same author, *Nationalism and Its Alternatives*, the populace of Italy, Spain, and Switzerland are each depicted as showing a common national consciousness, while specific references are also made to the successful assimilation of Bretons, Cornishmen, and Scots.

Nor were foreigners alone in their inability to anticipate recent developments. Thus in a 1967 work (Guy Heraud, *Peuples et Langues d'Europe*), a specialist on European minorities who was also a citizen of France asserted that the Corsicans are "profondément intégré à la nation française." Similarly, college textbooks written in the 1960s by such outstanding British specialists as S. E. Finer and Richard Rose tended to emphasize the absence of any politically significant cleavages in British society attributable to ethnic identity. Sometimes, members of a minority shared the inability to anticipate developments among their own people. As late as 1964, for example, a Scottish historian (J. D. Mackie, *A History of Scotland*) failed to detect the submerged but rapidly surfacing power of Scottish nationalism. And political leaders, if anything, proved less perspicacious than scholars. Today, the British Conservative Party is fervidly wooing the Scottish nationalists. But this courtship represents quite a *volte face* from 1967, when the Conservative Party's leader, Edward Heath, deprecatingly dismissed the nationalists as "flower people."

It is evident from the earlier quotations that one reason for the surprise engendered by the recent surge of ethnonationalism was a false image of Western Europe as a region devoid of significant national minorities. Benjamin Akzin (*State and Nation*, 1964) was articulating the conventional view of Western Europe when he noted: "If we look at the modern nation-states of Europe we shall see that, except perhaps for those of the Scandinavian peninsula, the population of each of them is largely the product of pre-existing ethnic groups which have integrated into the nations we know today. This is true of the French nation, consolidated from fairly hetero-geneous elements between the seventh and twelfth centuries. . . . Germans, Italians, Poles, Russians, and Spaniards have all become the well defined nations we know within a century or two of one another." In a similar vein, we read in Arnold Toynbee's monumental *A Study of History* (Vol. VIII, 1954) that "nationalism was comparatively innocuous in its West European birthplace, where, for the most part, it took the political map as it found it, and was content to utilize the existing parochial states, within their established frontiers, as its crucibles for the decoction of its intoxicating political brew of psychic energy." Within each state the populace came to be joined by "an inward sense of political solidarity springing from common political experiences, institutions, and ideals . . ."

This vision of Europe, of course, was based upon poor history. Rather than leaving the political map of Europe essentially untouched, ethno-nationalism, beginning with its first major manifestation at the time of the French Revolution, had given rise to an impressive series of challenges to the political map, many of which resulted in its redrawing. The Greek national war of liberation from the Ottoman Empire in the 1820s; the secession of the Flemings and Walloons from Dutch control in 1830; the abortive Polish uprisings against Russian domination between 1830-1832 and again in 1863; the similarly unsuccessful revolts throughout Europe in 1848 (particularly those involving the Italians, Hungarians, and Germans); the militarily achieved consolidation of Italy (1859-1870) and of Germany (1864-1871); the successful movement for the autonomy of Hungary in 1867; and the achievement of independence of Montenegro, Romania, and Serbia in 1878, of Norway in 1905, of Bulgaria in 1908, of Albania in 1912, of Finalnd in 1917, of Czechoslovakia, Estonia, Latvia, Lithuania, and Poland at the end of World War I (as well as the nine groups which seceded from Russia at this time only to be soon reabsorbed), of Ireland in 1921, of Iceland in 1944, of

Cyprus in 1960, and of Malta in 1964—all revolved about the ethnonational notion that a people should not be ruled by those deemed aliens.[1] If one were familiar with the manner in which the ethnonational virus had spread throughout Europe, why should he assume that the remaining minorities would prove mysteriously immune? Why should not the remaining minorities, many of whom are far more numerous than the Norse or Finns and most of whom are far more numerous than the Icelanders or Maltese, not be sufficiently influenced by these earlier movements to ask, "If them, why not us?" Carleton Hayes' thorough familiarity with the history of nationalism led him to raise just such questions. Four decades ago (*Essays on Nationalism*, 1926), he warned of potential troubles within Belgium and Switzerland, "despite the artificial attempts to promote a sense of social solidarity, akin to nationality, among all the Swiss and among all the Belgians." Elsewhere in the same work he referred to "the budding little nationalisms" of Basques, Catalans, Icelanders, Maltese, Manxmen, Wends, and White Russians.

Hayes' 1926 reference to "the budding nationalisms" of the time points up yet another way in which an inadequate regard for history helps to account for the general surprise which greeted the upsurge of ethnonationalism during the present decade. Most of the contemporary movements had a history transcending World War II, and some even World War I. (Remember, for example, that Napoleon, before becoming the leader of the French nation, had been an ardent champion of Corsican independence from Paris.) Several of these movements had their pre-World War II chroniclers; Shepard Clough's *A History of the Flemish Movement in Belgium: A Study in Nationalism* (1930) offers a case in point. But such studies were generally ignored in the postwar era. A great many well advertised, prewar portents were also ignored. Among them were (1) the voting of autonomy during the 1930s by Spanish Basques, Catalans, and Galicians; (2) the history of restiveness among the South Tyrolean Germans, commencing with their incorporation into Italy at the end of World War I and leading to the plebiscite ordered by Hitler, in which an astonishing number elected to leave their homes and settle within the Third Reich, rather than become Italian citizens, and leading in the immediate postwar era to a resumption of anti-state activities; (3) Hitler's successes in appealing to the ethnonational provlivities of Flemings and Bretons in order to get their collaboration; (4) Mussolini's similar appeal to the Corsicans; and (5) the separatist movements that were active in Sardinia and Sicily during the war and among the French-speaking Val d'Aostans both during and immediately following that same struggle.

The propensity to ignore such early indications of nationalism was not due simply to a poor level of awareness of prewar occurrences. Regardless of what had gone before, there was a general feeling in the afterglow of World War II that Europe, at least Western Europe, was on the threshold of a new, post-national age. The prewar primacy assigned to being French, Dutch, German, etc. was not held to have been succeeded, or at least was in the process of being succeeded, by a supranational consciousness of being European. In the words of Stanley Hoffman ("Obstinate or Obsolete: The Fate of the Nation-State" in *Conditions of World Order*, 1966):

> If there was one part of the world in which men of good will thought that the nation-state could be superseded, it was Western Europe. The conditions seemed ideal. On the one hand, nationalism seemed at its lowest ebb; on the other, an adequate formula and method for building a substitute had been devised.

That such a mood should prevail for a time throughout the region is quite understandable. The people were still recuperating from a holocaust whose principal casue was ethnonationalism in one of its most extreme forms. Stunned by the extravagant activities carried out in the name of a *Volksdeutsch* and a *razza italica*, it was to be expected that they would look somewhat suspiciously upon ethnonationalism in any form.

While this general reaction acted as a damper upon all such movements, certain groups were particularly enervated by it. Most significant was the impact that the recent equating of German nationalism with Naziism had upon pride in a German heritage. The impact has been quite apparent within Western Germany. With fresh memories of the unbridled passions proven to lurk in the Pandora's box of German nationalism; embarrassed by, if not remorseful for, the activities carried out in its name; realistically appraising postwar realities, particularly the presence of the Soviet Union in *Mittel Europa*; and aware that all non-German Europeans were vigilantly watching for the slightest symptom of a revitalization of German nationalism, German ethnonational proclivities were held in tight rein. The decreasing pride in a sense of Germanness, when Germanness was associated with Naziism, is illustrated by the Alsatians. Whereas the three political parties who favored autonomy for Alsace accounted for more than forty percent of the vote in 1928, such aspirations declined after the rise to power of Hitler, and had seemingly disappeared during the immediate postwar period. A similar development is evident in postwar Austria. Moreover, Naziism also exerted a special debilitating impact on ethnonational movements, such as those of the Flemings and Bretons, which had become tainted by collaborationism during the occupation. The immediate postwar period was one of quiessence for these movements which needed time for memories of such collaboration to fade, as well as time to replace its tainted elite, many of whom had fled, been killed by the underground, or incarcerated in the postwar period.

The psychological impact of World War II was destined to be fleeting, even within Western Germany. As memories fade, as the realization grows that

Naziism and German nationalism need not be synonomous, as pride of the postwar "economic miracle" takes on the hue of pride in German achievement, as older Germans come to believe that Germany's period of atonement and parole has lasted long enough, and as a postwar generation who believes it cannot be held in any way culpable for the mistakes of its parents comes into power, German nationalism manifests commensurate signs of recovery. Thus, in the 1972 elections, a party (the successful one), for the first time in the postwar period, pitched much of its sloganeering to national pride and consciousness. About this same time, stirrings of an ethnic coloration became visible among the Alsatians. For example a *Mouvement Regionaliste d'Alsace-Lorraine* was born in 1970. Flemings and Bretons, of course, had become active several years earlier.

With the advantage of hindsight, it now is clear that the image of Western Europeans as politically sophisticated cosmopolites who had come to recognize that nationalism was a dangerous anachronism in the modern age was always a heavily overdrawn one. It nevertheless required Charles de Gaulle's open appeals to *la grande nation* and *la gloire c'etait France* to dispel the illusion. A big factor in the creation of that illusion had been the move toward Western European integration. Did not the steps toward integration prove that the region's inhabitants had discarded narrow, ethnonational thinking? Again, this conclusion should have been tempered by the recollection that the driving force for regional integration had come not from cosmopolitanism but from a determination to safeguard against the phoenix-like resurrection of one of history's most fanatical manifestations of ethnonationalism run rampant (German Naziism). Regional integration was at least partly perceived as the price that must be paid to guarantee that the specter of a militant ethnonationalism still lurking under the surface was kept in check by making German capabilities (particularly those of a military nature) subject to a broader control-structure. Rather than developing from a cosmopolitan consensus, integrationist sentiment had developed precisely because Western Europe had been a cauldron of ethnic antagonisms and rivalries.

A second element to be considered in assessing the interrelationship between ethnonationalism and regional integration is that military and economic cooperation are not inconsistent with national consciousness, when the results of such cooperation are perceived as beneficial to the national interest. Thus, de Gaulle's nationalism did not blind him to the economic and prestige-related advantages that might accrue to *la grande nation* from membership in the European Economic Community (EEC). It did, on the other hand, cause him to shy from political integration and to demand *Europe des patries.* Moreover, the broad-scale toleration with which de Gaulle's insistence on a *Europe des patries* was greeted both within and without France suggested substantial though unarticulated support for the notion that any obituary for nationalism within Europe was premature.

Taken literally, a Europe of Fatherlands might appear to refer to a system based upon the primacy of ethnic homelands, but de Gaulle was well understood to mean, by "fatherlands," the present states. This formula serves well the national interest of those nations such as the English and French, who are clearly dominant in a large state, a factor which perhaps helps to explain London's willingness to enter the EEC only after becoming persuaded that the general drift of events was in accord with the de Gaulle formula. Already in a position to make the major decisions affecting the fate of their nation, these groups have not perceived so great a need for a more radical restructuring of the political system as have the minorities.

But somewhat ironically, the spokesmen for most of the region's ethnic minorities have also been amongst the most avid proponents of an integrated Western Europe.[2] The reasons for this support appear to be twofold. On the one hand, many of the minorities are either dissected by a political border or at least separated by one from a culturally akin people. Any development which tends to eradicate the barrier functions of the border thereby tends to unite or strengthen the nation. Thus, creation of the EEC has permitted closer ties between the French-speaking people on either side of the border between France and Italy's Val d'Aosta and between the Alsatians and Germans. Similarly, the co-entry of the United Kingdom and the Republic of Ireland held out the promise of closer ties between the people of the Republic and the Irish minority within Northern Ireland. So too, a reduction in the importance of present borders would permit closer association of the Bretons with their Celtic cousins in the United Kingdom and Ireland. This same motive is apparently behind the drive of the Basques and Catalans in promoting membership in the EEC for Spain and explains the South Tyroleans' desire for full membership (in place of the present special association) for Austria.

The second reason why the ethnic minorities support regional integration involves political alienation: since the particular state in which they find themselves is not perceived as the political expression of their own nation, the state's survival is not an emotional cause. More than this, the state has been seen as frustrating the nation's fundamental aspiration. Unlike, therefore, the English and French who presently dominate powerful states, the smaller and self-perceived politically dispossessed nations desire not a *Europe des patries* but a *Europe des ethnies*. The spokesmen for these peoples envisage a federated Europe composed of ethnically delineated states.

Whether these two views of an integrated Europe could be harmonized is extremely problematical. Our immediate point, however, is that the concept of *Europe des patries* and that of *Europe des ethnies* are both motivated by a desire to nurture and not to obliterate the national group. And regardless of which formula one favors, it is not at all clear why a regional structure should be expected to prove singularly immune to the challenge of ethnic aspirations which destroyed the multiethnic empires of yesterday and threatens the multiethnic states of today. The paradoxes are therefore numerous. But headlines reflecting regional integration should not be permitted to obscure the growing demands of the region's ethnic groups. More than a century ago, Lord Acton noted that "if we take the establishment of liberty for the realization of moral duties to be the end of civil society, we must conclude that those states are substantially the most perfect which, like the British and Austrian Empires, include various distinct nationalities without oppressing them." Yet neither of these multinational structures proved able to satisfy the ethnonational aspirations of its diverse peoples. Is there reason to believe that today's multinational states of Western Europe will prove more successful?

Notes

1. It is evident that many of the newly created states were themselves multinational. Such a state would be merely a step toward national self-determination, not its fulfillment. Multi-ethnic states were also created throughout Africa and Asia in the name of national self-determination. But as we are reminded by the abortive Biafran episode, the successful Bangladesh movement, and a host of current ethnic wars, one step toward self-determination is apt to be followed by demands for a further one.

2. The cool attitude of the Scottish National Party (SNP) toward membership in the EEC at the time of the British referendum on the question is only a partial exception. The SNP merely wanted to put off membership until Scotland could negotiate its own terms of entry.

Maria Borris

The Foreign Worker Problem
in the German Federal Republic

ECONOMIC CAUSES OF THE FOREIGN WORKER PROBLEM

AFTER the German Democratic Republic in 1961 had brought migration of labor to a halt by building the wall straight through Berlin and by imposing rigorous border controls, the Federal Republic tried to replenish its labor force by bringing immigration from the Mediterranean countries under a central control.[1] These countries have remained the main source of immigration up to the present time, although their quotas have been switched during this period. At first the Italians formed the largest group, but they have now been overtaken by the Turks, followed by the Yugoslavs. The switching resulted from changes made in agreements between the German central labor office and the governments of these countries—known as the "third countries"—and from the changing economic conditions, especially in Italy whose inhabitants enjoy freedom of movement as part of the European Economic Community.

Undoubtedly migration was determined by an increasing demand for labor in the Federal Republic at a time of irregular but considerable rates of economic growth in the post-war period: a situation which led to the assumption that economic growth is constantly linked with increasing employment, although investment in rationalization meant replacing human labor by machinery. This mistaken assumption led to the fear that the economic growth necessitated by international economic competition and by a home policy aimed at social stability might be slowed down through a shortage of indigenous labor or that the increasing numbers of foreign workers would make far too great demands on the possibilities of regional

9

planning in regard to the economic and social substructures.

In face of this ominous dilemma the federal government and some of the *Land* governments had recourse to expert opinions forecasting future economic growth as growth of the social product and of the labor force required in given periods of time. But in all these expert opinions the growth rates of the social product were constantly underestimated and the share of the indigenous population in the gain overestimated. The earnings ratio of women declined or stagnated instead of increasing and the raising of the school-leaving age further postponed the age of starting work. Consequently the estimates of the numbers of foreigners employed varied for the years 1975, 1980, and 1985. These forecasts merely projected past sequences of development into the future, without paying sufficient attention to technical, scientific, economic, social, and internal political changes. Existing production structures and the previous demand for labor were simply extended into the future, in the hope apparently that everything would go on as before.

Nevertheless the unperceived changes in the rates of capital accumulation at home and the reasons for a readiness to invest superfluous indigenous capital abroad were factors in the uncertainty which led the federal government finally in 1973 to reverse its immigration policy. By January 1973 the number of foreign workers had risen to 2.35 million. In November of the same year recruitment of workers was stopped and has not been resumed up to the present time. The federal government let it be known that the stop would not be relaxed even in the future, despite the appearance of a boom in the economy. The reasons for this attitude were evidently the fact that there were almost a million unemployed and the prediction that the boom could be accompanied by a persistently high upper limit to the number of unemployed German workers.

It seems as if the government wanted to bring pressure to bear on the acceleration of rationalization in industry, on the assumption that suitable jobs would be created for German workers and that there would be less need of uneducated foreign workers. It was made known however, especially from industry and the public service sector, according to press reports, that the building industry as well as the automobile and electrical industries could not completely dispense with foreign workers. It is estimated that up to 1.5 to 1.8 million foreigners will still be needed in the coming years. This information may well encourage plans for letting the previous immigrants—especially those with families—return to their home countries, for recruiting younger workers without families or preventing the entry of families and introducing a strict rotation after two to three years (a policy which had hitherto been rejected as inhuman).

These considerations clearly show that foreign labor forms a disposable reserve army which is to be used as desired in the light of economic and social necessities. The integration of parts of the foreign population, especially of those who had lived more than five years in the Federal Republic and who possessed a right to a residence permit according to the aliens law, propagated up to 1972, is to be reversed. For this however a change in the law would be needed, but it is not yet known when or whether it will come about.

CONCENTRATION AND SEGREGATION OF FOREIGN WORKERS[2]

The problem of the concentration and segregation of foreign workers and their families—especially in the industrially congested areas of the large cities and regions of Rhein-Main, Baden-Württemberg, Nordrhein-Westfalen—will remain ever under any new ruling; in fact, it will become more acute, since it is probable that men and women on their own working in the Federal Republic will be accommodated in mass quarters or in communes, separated from the German population. *The problem of concentration and segregation is more qualitative than quantitative.* It can affect a million and a half just as closely as two million and a half; it can touch them even more harshly if they have to live in Western Germany without their families. *They are legally an under-privileged minority* since their rights are restricted by the aliens law of 1965. A more liberal solution has been accepted since 1961 for members of the European communities, based on the principles of the Common Market Regulation 1612 of 1968, which permits them freedom of movement in the Federal Republic and expressly permits entry at their own risk. But the economic crisis of 1974/1975 showed that Italian workers became unemployed just like those from the "third countries" and then returned to Italy as soon as their claim to unemployment pay had run out.

From the very outset *the object of the aliens law was to protect Germans against foreigners* and to maintain the priority of national interests; the latter however were not defined more closely and consequently could be given very arbitrary interpretations. It allows only a limited residence permit, restricting the person to certain places and certain callings. If the legal provisions are infringed, if a penal offense is committed or if dependence on social welfare (in the form guaranteed for disabled persons, old people, children, or German nationals in need) goes on too long, they can be expelled. Such a restriction on the scope of freedom in itself always made integration into the German population difficult, particularly since the authorities are not bound by any precise rules.

Consequently foreigners live in a state of legal insecurity: they cannot make any long-term plans and must therefore be in constant fear for their livelihood—a state of affairs which, as is well known, can seriously affect a person's health. Statistics suggest that the incidence of sickness is not greater, but in fact even less among foreign workers than among Germans, which may be due to the more favourable age composition of the foreign population. The conclusions of surveys however show that psychosomatic illnesses arising from stress, loneliness, unhappiness and insecurity are more prevalent.

As far as the laws in regard to work and social welfare are concerned, foreign workers are on the same plane as Germans. This is the result of intervention by the trade unions seeking to protect German employees from cheap labor, not paid according to the wage scale. But that is not to say that they receive the same wages as the Germans for the same jobs, since wage scales in the Federal Republic represent only minimum wages: effective wages differ from these in varying degrees in the different wage groups. The provisions of the law for promoting employment, the regulations on work permits and a separate ruling by the Federal Labor Institute of November 1974 all aim at relieving the social services of the obligation to support workers no longer needed as a result of the economic and social crisis of the years 1974/1975/1976.

The dual controls of work and residence permits favors segregation. Restriction of political rights has the same effect: the prohibition by the ruling of the aliens' authorities (Section 6 of the aliens law) of political activity, if required by "important interests of the German Federal Republic." Freedom of opinion is restricted and there is no right to elect or to be elected. These restrictions have been publicly opposed by the Christian churches, charitable organizations, humanitarian associations, the trade unions, and some lawyers, but without any visible success. While there was a tendency as late as 1970/1971 to liberalize the aliens law, the opposite trend set in even before the economic crisis. It is not clear whether this was because of terrorism, but it is quite possible, since the law holds for all foreign nationals and not only for immigrants seeking work. It should however be regarded as merely the framework for segregation and defective integration; for the opportunities are no better even for Italians, although Italy belongs to the European Community.

Segregation is a consequence of the inferior social status of foreign workers. They are engaged on work requiring minimal qualifications, which German workers are not willing to undertake even during the crisis, although the Federal Labor Institute—with some protests from the unions—has tried to interpret very broadly the idea of the acceptability of certain forms of work. The federal government cannot risk any tightening in the application of the conditions of employment before the elections in October 1976. Both the restrictions on recruitment and the plans to force the return of the immigrants serve in the last resort to pacify the German workers who—as surveys show—largely assume that the presence of foreign workers is the cause of their own unemployment: which can scarcely be the case, since the foreigners work on jobs which the Germans spurn. This view of things betrays the ignorance on the part of the German workers of the real reasons for the economic crisis and their aversion to foreign workers which exists even in times of propsperity, an aversion which makes social contacts difficult or even impossible and finds expression in a variety of terms of abuse (layabouts, stinkers, riffraff, swine). The German workers avoid the company of the foreigners outside the factory and even inside isolate themselves at the midday lunchtime interval in the canteens. They rationalize this behaviour by referring to the foreigners' limited knowledge of German. In fact the investigation already mentioned, in Frankfurt/Main, showed that the very opposite was the case: it was not their limited knowledge of German which caused the isolation, but segregation which caused them to have only a limited knowledge of German. A large proportion of the foreign workers did not want to learn German because they had no opportunity to speak it.

HOUSING SITUATION OF THE FOREIGNERS[3]

Isolation from the Germans leads to a retreat into the ethnic group, into the family. It is true that there are not yet any ghettos in the Federal Republic, except in Berlin where the Kreuzberg district forms a Turkish ghetto. In other large cities, in areas where Germans live or among blocks of houses partly occupied by a variety of foreign groups, whole streets have emerged with an exclusively foreign population. These are mostly areas with badly equipped homes, in the city centers abandoned by more affluent members of the population, in working-class areas with old buildings or in broken-down houses owned by members of the lower middle class. Such houses are not renovated because much more money can be made from the high rents than by selling them to Germans, after renovation, at market prices. Speculation in land in the large cities also led to buying up whole groups of houses which were then left to become dilapidated through being overcrowded with foreign families—until fresh building on a large scale could be made profitable for commercial use.

This speculation was brought to an end too late by the provisions of the law for urban planning; this occurred mostly only when public attention was drawn to the destruction of urban areas, as a result of the defensive action of the citizens in what were known as citizens' initiatives, the Frankfurt movement becoming famous in other European countries. It has not hitherto been possible anywhere to alleviate the housing needs of foreign families, although the public authorities have made an effort to eliminate the worst conditions. Steps have been taken against people drawing exorbitant rents; nevertheless many foreigners hesitate to report these things and to become involved in a legal wrangle with the landlords, out of fear that this will be recorded by the authorities. This is in fact an unreal fear, but one which is typical of their psychological and social condition.

THE SITUTATION OF FOREIGN CHILDREN

According to the Educational Acts of the federal lands the children must attend German schools as long as German children do. But, since their knowledge of the language is inadequate for following instruction, they are temporarily instructed in national classes by teachers of their own nationality, paid by the German educational authorities, and follow syllabuses supervised by the German authorities and the foreign consulates. This cooperation functioned very badly in the past with states not ruled by democratically elected governments, since no agreement could be reached on syllabuses and the content of the teaching.

Classes in the schools are mostly overcrowded; the children cannot do their homework on their own. They have to repeat the lessons and are quite often sent to special schools for handicapped children, although they show no signs of being educationally subnormal. Friendly contact with German children is often lacking and German parents complain to the educational authorities that their children will receive inadequate instructions when the number of foreign pupils amounts to a third of the whole. Admittedly foreign parents want an integration of their children, since they themselves are living in isolation, but they are often put off again by their experience of the schools. So there arises an inconsistent attitude to the German school, which remains alien to them as an institution although many of them attend parents' evenings and take an interest in what happens to their children in school. Youth centers established in many towns and cities are open also to foreign children in their leisure time; but the latter seldom visit them and then only in groups within which they feel that they are protected. International youth conventions organized annually by the authorities together with teachers and social workers have been widely approved, but they have not been able to create a basis for permanent contact. This failure is also linked with the crisis of German youth work, whether organized by communal centers, voluntary youth associations, or charitable organizations.

POSSIBILITIES OF INTEGRATION?

The question has been discussed among sociologists as to whether the very fact of being crowded in ghettos, in living quarters, itself prevents integration, since it is here that a national or ethnic cohesion again takes shape and frustrates any desire for integration. Foreign workers, like any other types of minorities, can satisfy their social needs in this situation, while the mere fact of living dispersed among the majority would itself facilitate or even perhaps create integration. The simple distribution of foreign workers in the different parts of a town or city however has no effect on integration. Even their share in social-political services which are also at the disposal of the German population—national health insurance, protection of working mothers, accident insurance, social insurance—and their participation in the rights of the employees within the factory laws, their eligibility for the works council, have resulted in integration for individuals, but not for the majority of foreign workers as a whole.

Social integration—which can of course only be integration into the

German working class—has not been effected. In public only legal integration, including the right to elect and to be elected, has been discussed, at least in the Christian church communities and charitable organizations, in the trade unions, who compiled all the memoranda and passed them on to the federal government or to the Ministry for Labor and Social Order. Mainly for economic reasons, but also because of internal political considerations, these had no effect. Consequently efforts in this direction have been confined to the many official and informal initiative committees in which foreign associations or groups or individual delegates took part and which developed a series of activities to take into their permanent care individual families looking for help, or persons or groups, young people in particular, with financial assistance from the Federal Labor Institute, the social ministries of the lands, the Federal Labor Ministry or the local authorities.

The primary aim was to help them to preserve their national or ethnic identity, so that they could then enter confidently into contact with German groups, who would facilitate their integration into the different strata of the working class. But in fact these attempts to preserve national identity— cultivation of the mother tongue, certain national customs, folk-singing and dancing—have had the very opposite effect: a definite retreat into the national or ethnic group. For these expressions of the national cultures were so remote from the habits of a German urban population that their sole effect was occasionally to impress the German workers with their exotic charm. Despite all the good intentions, what has happened hitherto has not made life any easier for foreigners in an alien milieu which has never welcomed them from the very beginning of the immigration.

Notes
1. Cf., on this section, G. Schiller, "Arbeitskraftreserven (Perspektiven und Entwicklung)" in a special number of *Die Dritte Welt*, Meisenheim, 1975, pp. 250-269.
2. Cf. M. Borris, *Ausländische Arbeiter in einer Grossstadt*, Frankfurt/Main, 1974²; cf. Bingemer, Meistermann-Seeger, Neubert, *Leben als Gastarbeiter (Geglückte oder missglückte Integration)*, Cologne and Opladen, 1970.
3. Schöfl, Strunk, Tonne, *Untersuchung zur Wohnsituation ausländischer Arbeiter in Baden-Württemberg*, Stuttgart, 1972; cf. E. Zieris, *Wohnverhältnisse von Familien ausländischer Arbeitnehmer in Nordrhein-Westfalen*, NRW, 1971.

John Simpson

Ethnic Groups and Church Attendance in the United States and Canada

ONE of the more prominent formulations in the field of ethnic studies in the United States is the Herberg thesis linking the Americanization of immigrant groups and their descendants with generation specific patterns of church attendance.[1] Herberg argued that the children of immigrants (second generation) turn away from the church but a renewed interest occurs among members of the third generation. The pattern predicted by Herberg was based on four assumptions: (1) the existence of social pressure on immigrants to assimilate and become Americanized; (2) diminishing religious activity in the second generation because of (a) alienation from the ethnic church and (b) uneasiness with the non-ethnic church due to incomplete assimilation; (3) the adoption of the "American Way of Life" including the practice of religion by the third generation; (4) replacement of an ethnic group identity by a religious identity (Protestant-Catholic-Jew) among members of the third generation.

While Herberg never empirically tested his thesis, others have investigated it.[2] Although the findings are not consistent with the exact pattern predicted by Herberg, they do suggest that the process of Americanization and the practice of religion may be linked for some Roman Catholics and Protestants. Among Roman Catholics, without taking into consideration ethnic background, church attendance increases with each successive generation. Among Protestants, the third generation attends more frequently than the first generation with the second generation either attending as frequently or more frequently than the first generation depending upon the set of data examined. With ethnic background taken into consideration, the available data indicate either no significant change in church attendance over three generations (Irish

16

Table I—Percentage Attending Church Frequently*

ETHNIC GROUP	COUNTRY	RELIGIOUS AFFILIATION	GENERATION		
			1	2	3
Dutch	Canada	Protestant	65% (99)	33% (36)	32% (37)
Scandanavian	Canada	Protestant	34% (59)	26% (86)	22% (45)
Ukrainian	Canada	Ukrainian Catholic	69% (39)	60% (30)	47% (15)
German	Canada	Protestant	49% (99)	46% (52)	49% (57)
German	Canada	Roman Catholic	67% (32)	50% (12)	64% (22)
German**	U.S.A.	Roman Catholic	50% (10)	83% (70)	93% (135)
Italian	Canada	Roman Catholic	57% (244)	55% (58)	38% (8)a
Italian**	U.S.A.	Roman Catholic	72% (25)	66% (235)	67% (48)
Polish	Canada	Roman Catholic	63% (70)	55% (53)	54% (28)
Polish**	U.S.A.	Roman Catholic	60% (5)a	80% (107)	79% (48)
(not controlled)	Canada	Protestant	51% (328)	30% (263)	35% (197)
(not controlled)	Canada	Ukrainian Catholic	70% (40)	59% (34)	50% (20)
(not controlled)	Canada	Roman Catholic	58% (570)	53% (173)	48% (88)

Except for the rows in which a double asterisk occurs, the entries in this table result from the analysis of data gathered in 1973 under the auspices of the Secretary of State, Ottawa. A stratified random sample of those whose mother tongue or ancestral mother tongue is neither French nor English was drawn from five cities: Montreal, Toronto, Winnipeg, Edmonton, and Vancouver. Of the ten groups surveyed, four—Greek, Hungarian, Portuguese, and Chinese—are not analyzed in this paper because the size of the group in the sample is too small. The author is grateful to Professor Jeffrey G. Reitz, University of Toronto, for making the data available. Further information is available in K. G. O'Bryan, J. G. Reitz, and O. Kuplowsky, *Non-Official Languages In Canada*, (Ottawa, 1975).

*For the Canadian data the percentages represent those who say they attend church once a month or more. For the American data the percentages are those who report weekly Mass attendance.

**The entries in these rows are taken from Harold J. Abramson, *Ethnic Diversity In Catholic America*, (New York, 1973), p. 115.

aPercentage may be unreliable because of the number of cases on which it is based.

and Italian) or a significant increase (Polish and German) among Roman Catholics of European extraction.

Table 1 contains church attendance data for a sample of ethnic groups in Canada and some comparable American data. In Canada church attendance tends to either remain the same or decline in frequency among ethnic groups over three generations. Furthermore, when ethnicity is not taken into consideration there is a generational decline among those of similar religious affiliation.

Thus, the available data indicate that the frequency of church attendance over three generations among ethnic groups in the United States either remains constant or increases. In Canada, on the other hand, the frequency of church attendance declines among most ethnic groups or remains constant. These patterns, it will be argued, are consistent with differences in the nature of pluralism in the two countries and, especially, with differences in the articulation of the individual's religious and ethnic identity with the symbols of nationhood.

THE AMERICAN MELTING POT AND THE CANADIAN MOSAIC

Both Canada and the United States have been populated by immigrants, most of them from the United Kingdom and Europe, who have become citizens of their new country. In the process of nation building, however, different patterns of dealing with immigrants emerged in the two societies. Thus, it is common to speak of the United States as a "melting pot" and Canada as a "mosaic." The melting pot metaphor conveys the image of a socially homogenous society populated by a new cultural type—the American—formed by fusing together the cultural traits of all immigrants. The mosaic refers to a pluralistic nation in which immigrants are politically and economically integrated but maintain their own distinctive cultures based on the language and customs of the country of origin. While the melting pot and mosaic are rhetorical idealizations, they, nevertheless, suggest that important differences have existed between the United States and Canada in the treatment of immigrants.[3]

An immigrant to the United States has always been faced with the problem of becoming an American. The pressure to Americanize rests upon the fundamental premise that the United States is a new creation vis-à-vis European culture and institutions. While continuities existed between the republic and Europe, forming a new nation by revolution and the construction of an institutional framework for government and a common life left an enduring legacy of the sense that to become an American is to participate in a new order. For the individual the new order provided a new identity—American—which the immigrant was expected to acquire.

While Americanization was the norm, it is clearly the case that not all immigrants were thoroughly Americanized. As studies indicate, ethnicity continues to persist in American life as an important focus of identity, organization, and action.[4] Furthermore, Americanization, when it did occur, meant absorbing the values and cultural patterns of the once overwhelmingly dominant Anglo-Saxon Americans and not adhering to a culture produced in a melting pot which has never existed.

Perhaps, the single most important source of pressure to Americanize has been the unfaltering rhetorical reinforcement by political and economic elites of the belief that there is something called "The American Way of Life" and that it is possible to become an American. The ideology of Americanism has meant that the maintenance of ethnic identity in the United States must be achieved within a cultural milieu which, historically, has been more hostile than not to the expression of ethnicity.[5]

In contrast with the United States, the development of Canada as a nation has been marked by a series of events which resulted in the promotion of ethnic pluralism as a significant feature of national life. The primary source of this outcome was the settlement worked out between the British and the French remaining in North America following the end of French rule in 1763. Although the British gained military and political control, the French in Quebec were allowed, as a practical matter, to maintain their religion and language. Thus, the precedent was set in British North America for the maintenance of ethnicity within the framework of British colonial sovereignty and the evolution of a national politics in which reconciling the interests of different language groups would play an important role.

The American Revolution, itself, contributed to the development of Canadian multi-culturalism since a significant number of Loyalists migrated north into the area remaining under British control. They brought with them an identity founded upon loyalty to the Crown of England, thereby deliberately shunning a new identity based upon the rejection of the Old World. Furthermore, the desire of French, English, Irish, and Scottish groups to remain separate contributed to the formation of a tradition of ethnic group loyalty. Future immigrants would find no common Canadian identity to substitute for their entrance identity since none had been forged in the development of the nation. No "Canadian Way of Life" awaited venturers to the shores of Canada. Rather they were faced with the task of adapting to their new environment, while adhering to ethnic symbols and practices.

PLURALISM AND RELIGIOUS PRACTICE IN NORTH AMERICA

What is the meaning of religious practice within American pluralism in tension with an assimilationist milieu and Canadian pluralism more favorably oriented to the expression of ethnicity? The major difference between the United States and Canada in this regard is that unlike the United States, it is difficult in Canada for an individual to articulate the practice of religion with national identity, that is with "being Canadian."

While some denominations in the United States emphasize an ethnic orientation, the larger denominations are ethnically non-exclusive. The absence of a strong unified ethnic emphasis within these denominations, however, does not mean that they have ceased to perform organized religion's tradational function of providing adherents with a sense of participation in peoplehood. For in the context of the denominational organization of religion, an ideology exists which strongly associates Judeo-Christian symbols with the idea of America.[6] Thus, it is possible for an individual to interpret his practice of religion as participation in "The American Way of Life." While religion is not established in the United States, the value placed upon religious practice as part of "The American Way of Life" means that church attendance can be interpreted as a patriotic act. As former President Eisenhower said, "Our government makes no sense unless it is founded in a deeply felt religious faith...."[7] Between the denominations there are, of course, differences and conflicts, yet all may see themselves as supporting the idea of America.

In the absence of strong and long-lasting attempts to efface ethnicity, the tie between religious practice and ethnic identity has remained firmer in Canada than in the United States. Within many Canadian denominations a sense of peoplehood exists which is continuous with some European or British past. For example, among Protestants the Anglican and Presbyterian bodies are rooted in ethnic and class divisions which existed within the United Kingdom and may still be used by adherents, today, to distinguish themselves from others in Canada.

Complementing the relatively close tie between ethnicity and religious practice in Canada is the absence of a patriotic rhetoric linking religious practice with the symbols of nationhood. God and the flag do not go along as nicely together in Canada as they do in the United States. While both the United States and Canada prohibit the formal establishment of any religion, in Canada there is no symbolic establishment of the virtue of religious practice as there is in the United States. This important difference between the two nations is largely due to the failure of Protestant evangelicals in Canada to impose a consensus at the national level containing their working assumptions that religion should be voluntaristic and designed to meet spiritual needs derived from an ideology of individualism.[8] The major obstacle, of course, was the political reality of Quebec in which the practice of religion—Roman Catholicism—was strongly linked with a collective purpose: the desire of the Quebecois to maintain themselves as a people in the presence of English dominance.

Although close ties may exist in Canada between the affirmation of specific ethnic traditions and the practice of religion, the feeling and expression of ethnicity do not necessarily depend upon the practice of religion. In Canada the accomodation of immigrants is marked over generations by less involvement in all ethnic organizations including churches while a positive orientation to ethnic roots is maintained.[9] Thus while a personal sense of ethnic identity remains, over generations religious practice may decline due to the influence of secularizing forces which are not mitigated by the idea that one can be a good Canadian by going to church.

Furthermore, since there is no strong tradition of negatively defining ethnicity as part of a process of Canadianization, religious practice is not likely to become a substitute for the expression of ethnicity. Therefore, it is not surprising that, as Table 1 indicates, the frequency of church attendance over three generations among the ethnic groups in Canada for which there are data does not increase. In fact, decreases occur in most cases. The data in Table 1 are consistent with the absence of a link in Canada between the practice of religion and the identification of the individual with the nation, a link which has existed in the United States.

HERBERG RECONSIDERED

There can be little doubt that Herberg was wrong on some points and overstated his case on others. The prediction of high first generation attendance, low second generation attendance, and high third generation attendance is not supported by the evidence. Furthermore, the idea of a triple melting pot with a religious identity invariably being substituted in the third generation for an ethnic identity, is suspect because church attendance patterns differ among those with the same religious affiliation but different ethnic origins. Despite these shortcomings, however, the Herberg thesis is still important because it recognizes that a relationship may exist between the Americanization of immigrants and church attendance. The data in Table 1 and elsewhere are consistent with the interpretation that while some ethnic groups may be less susceptible to the pressure to Americanize and, therefore, not change their church attendance patterns, others may become Americanized and attend church more frequently. Furthermore, in Canada, which resembles the United States more than any other nation in the world but provides no Canadian identity which can be affirmed by church attendance, the tendency to go to church declines or remains constant over generations. Taken together, Canada and the United States provide something resembling a controlled experiment in which other important factors are held constant while the existence of a national identity and pressure upon immigrants to acquire it are varied. That being the case, the data in Table 1 are not inconsistent with Herberg's insight regarding the relationship between Americanization and church attendance.

Will the observed pattern persist? The Herberg thesis has not been assessed with nationally representative data gathered in the United States after 1964. Since then some central elements in the idea of America have been seriously called into question. Black protest, Vietnam, and Watergate undermined important parts of American mythology. Black protest raised questions about domestic freedom and equal opportunity for all. Vietnam destroyed the myth of the nation as a peace-loving, benign defender of freedom and democracy in the world. Finally, Watergate damaged the confidence of the nation in its own righteousness as a land removed, at the highest levels of office, from the corruption and intrigue of the rest of the world.

What can be said about the tie between denominational religion and American identity in light of the corroded myth of America? Essentially, the Sixties forced upon the national consciousness a reinterpretation of the idea of America which was thoroughly inconsistent with the minimal ethical demands of denominational religion. An enormous chasm was opened between what religion was supposed to stand for and the perceived behaviour of the nation, thereby placing a severe strain upon the notion of participating in America through the practice of religion.

It is, of course, too early to assess with any degree of certainty the eventual outcome of the myth-destroying events of the Sixties. It would appear to be the case, however, that the American solution to the problem of creating an ideology of national unity out of ethnic and religious diversity has been dealt a severe blow.

Notes
1. Will Herberg, *Protestant-Catholic-Jew* (Garden City, New York, 1960).
2. Gerhard Lenski, *The Religious Factor* (Garden City, New York, 1963); Bernard Lazerwitz and Louis Rowitz, "The Three Generation Hypothesis," *American Journal of Sociology* 69 (1964), pp. 529–538; Bernard Lazerwitz, "Contrasting the Effects of Generation, Class, Sex, and Age on Group Identification in the Jewish and Protestant Communities," *Social Forces* 49 (1970), pp. 50–59; Harold J. Abramson, *Ethnic Diversity in Catholic America* (New York, 1973); Hart M. Nelsen and H. D. Allen, "Ethnicity, Americanization, and Religious Attendance," *American Journal of Sociology* 79 (1974), pp. 906–922.
3. Allan Smith, "Metaphor and Nationality in North America," *Canadian Historical Review* 51 (1970), pp. 247–275.
4. Among the more important studies are Nathan Glazer and Daniel Patrick Moynihan, *Beyond the Melting Pot* (Cambridge, Massachusetts, 1963) and Andrew M. Greeley, *Ethnicity in the United States* (New York, 1974).
5. John Higham, *Strangers In The Land* (New York, 1963).
6. Robert N. Bellah, "Civil Religion in America," *Daedalus*, (Winter 1967), pp. 1–21.
7. *The New York Times*, December 23, 1952.
8. John Webster Grant, " 'At Least You Knew Where You Stood With Them': Reflections On Religious Pluralism in Canada and the United States," *Studies In Religion* 2 (1973), pp. 340–351.
9. Jeffrey G. Reitz, "Language and Ethnic Community Survival," *Canadian Review of Sociology and Anthropology*, Special Issue (1974), pp. 102–124.

Michel de Verteuil, Henry Charles and Clyde Harvey

West Indies:
Old Nations and New Nations

I

BETWEEN 1492 and 1504, Christopher Columbus claimed for Spain a group of islands in the Western Hemisphere, stretching from Cuba in the north to Trinidad in the south. The islands, together with some sections of the South American mainland, came to be known as the Caribbean, the Antilles or the West Indies. Covering some 200,000 square miles and with a population of nine million people, they include Spanish, French, Dutch and English-speaking peoples, independent nations and small dependencies, modernized states and subsistence economies.

In this essay we shall consider only the former English colonies of the Caribbean. Some of these, e.g., Barbados, Grenada, Guyana, Jamaica, Trinidad and Tobago, are now politically independent states; others, e.g. St. Lucia, have a relationship of associated statehood with Britain whereby they tend to their own affairs internally while Britain retains responsibility for foreign affairs and defence. Together they have a population of over four million people. Guyana excluded (83,000), they cover some 25,000 square miles.

The Spaniards came in search of the wealth of the Indies. They found here two groups of Amerindian peoples, the mild and pacific Arawaks and the fiercer Caribs. Thanks to the Papal Donation of 1493, they had a monopoly of exploration and colonization in the region. Where possible, they subdued the indigenous Amerindians, forcing them to work the plantations. However, the subsequent discoveries on the mineral-rich mainland in Peru and Mexico quickly diverted Spanish attention from the islands and few colonies actually

23

prospered. These discoveries also attracted other European nations. Spain's hegemony in Europe was already being seriously challenged by the Dutch, English and French, and this challenge had repercussions in the West Indies. By the early seventeenth century the Dutch had become a power in the region concentrating mainly on trade rather than settlement, the British had colonies in Jamaica, Guyana and the Lesser Antilles, while the French had settled Hispaniola, Guadeloupe and Martinique. Most of the smaller colonies changed hands more than once, making for a rich diversity within the colonies themselves, a cultural situation which exists to this day.

It was these non-Hispanic colonies which initiated the first significant migrations to the region. Originally tobacco growers, the colonists soon turned to sugar which required a large, strong but unskilled labor force. At first this was supplied by indentured labor and then by convict labor from Europe, but neither source could ensure a steady supply. So the colonizers turned to African slave labor which was to flourish in the region until the mid-nineteenth century. Most of these slaves came from the west coast of Africa and were intended for North and South America as well.

Slavery for the Africans meant complete disorientation from their homeland and traditions. A slave had no right to family ties or religious expression. His only social identity was that of slave subject to his white master. Slavery created in the Caribbean a society based on race and economic relations, with the rich white master and the poor black slave at either extreme and with various gradations of color and economic standing in between as determinants of social position.

The emancipation of the slaves (in 1838 for the British colonies, 1848 for the French and 1863 for the Dutch) led to a change in attitude on the part of the slaves. They no longer wanted to work on the plantations, and this led to the introduction of other groups into the society. Unsuccessful attempts were made to introduce Chinese and Portuguese labor, but the most significant of all the new workers were the indentured laborers from India who were brought in large numbers to Trinidad, Guyana and Surinam. These came to work for limited periods after which they were either to be repatriated or given small plots of land to cultivate. They brought with them a strong sense of family as well as definite religious traditions, predominantly Hindu. Unlike the slaves, they were allowed to retain their religious and social identity.

The Caribbean today is a mixture of these racial groupings in an economic and social system which still bears the marks of the experience of slavery and is best described as a plantation economy. All the islands are heavily dependent on agriculture, either as the biggest source of revenue or as the main labor market. The descendants of the Europeans still dominate the business sector, although political power lies in the hands of a black, university-educated elite in most places. In the majority of the islands people of African descent number over 80% of the population. In Guyana, East

Indians are 55%, while in Trinidad they are slightly less than 50%. In both these countries they play a significant role in the economic, political and religious life of the country.

II

Each metropolitan culture-system in the area left its special mark upon its colonial subjects. Together these systems bequeathed to Caribbean society the legacy of imperialism, remote political and economic control, slavery, indentureship, cultural domination, discrimination by race and color, and extreme fragmentation at the level of the community, the nation and the region.

Life in the Caribbean still represents the difficult task of coming to terms with this history and overcoming its effects.

Like most other colonial peoples, shorn of their self-confidence, the Caribbean peoples were until recently not anxious to survey their past experiences and contemplate their history. If culture is also a people's self-estimation, the memory of what they have been and the potentialities of which they are capable, Caribbean culture remained until relatively recently self-deprecatory, if not actually self-ashamed. There was the endemic feeling that nothing good had come or could come from the region or its people. It was a society, in a Trinidadian phrase, "good for nothing," importing its identity along with trade and living in virtual schizophrenia.

The region was not unaffected by the modern upsurge in self-awareness among formerly colonized peoples. Recent years have seen new movements emerging in the islands, probing new frontiers in the search for the development of a society which is responsible, true to itself, socially equal and authentic. The consensus has grown that solutions for regional ills must begin in the minds of Caribbean peoples themselves and from a recognition of the reality in which they live. It is romantic to hanker after ancestral roots either in Africa or India as the sole foundation on which to erect national identity or build regional hope.

What pervades the region today is a mood of careful optimism and a growing sense of future possibilities. Not without the fear of failure, however. Political federation came to nothing in the 1960s and economic federation proceeds shakily in the 70s. In some islands governments have moved to curtail individual and social liberties, silencing opposition by force and restricting avenues of public criticism. Necessary legislation for promoting healthier family living and providing points of growth for the better evolution of family life patterns in the region is yet to be enacted and implemented on a wide scale. High levels of unemployment remain even in the relatively better islands like Jamaica and Trinidad; poverty is everywhere.

It is not difficult to understand the character of the new regional movements, all of them populist in inspiration. Caribbean peoples have historically existed only at the periphery of their own existence, and considered less important than either commerce or profit. Unlike emancipation, independence has meant little more than the redefinition of legal status, not bringing in its wake any great metamorphosis.

The future rests largely with the young. In many of the islands about 60% of the total population is less than 25 years of age. Brought up in a milieu different from that of their parents and uninhibited by the psychological and social complexes that distorted the lives of many of the older folk, they are seeking to establish the indigenous basis for a better society in the future.

Basic threats, both internal and external, still remain. Internally, a voluntarism with little basis either in rationality or in history, going hand in hand with a disregard for discipline and the ability to take pains; externally, there remains the threat of cultural and economic absorption by powerful North America.

III

The religious faith of the peoples of the Caribbean is as pluralist as their history and their culture. This makes speech about the situation very difficult. One must always make distinctions and put limits to one's conclusions.

Though it is true that Christians are in the majority, there are large numbers of Hindus and Muslims, particularly in Guyana and Trinidad, as mentioned earlier, where they make up more than one third of the population. As can be expected, there has been little interchange between them and the Christian churches. Hindus and Muslims have maintained their religious practices in an unbroken way. The Hindus in particular have been influenced by their history in the Caribbean but up to now have not attempted to identify the distinctive characteristics of their religion in this setting.

Then there are the African religions, or rather the amalgam of African religions and Christianity which emerged from the African experience in the Caribbean. Here too, there is a living faith, though it is difficult to assess its vitality since many of the adherents of these religions are also adherents of one or another of the Christian churches.

As in other countries there is the important distinction between the more structured churches, like the Anglican, the Catholic and the Presbyterian, and the "free churches" or sects, Baptist, Pentecostal and others. One finds, then, two forms of Christianity, very different in structure, spirit and practice, and playing different roles in society. The distinction has, moreover, clear class connotations; the more structured churches are considered to have status, while the free churches are considered the province of the poor and the less educated.

Looking at the established churches, one finds that they have one thing in common, and that is that they accepted practically without question the models of church life received from the parent churches; few if any concessions were made to local conditions. And this was true not only of a highly centralized church like the Catholic Church, but of the others as well. A good example is the use of symbols. The religious symbols of Caribbean Christian churches are all European. Jesus and the Virgin Mary are portrayed as Europeans with the minor variation that in Hollywood films (an important factor in shaping religious sensibilities here) they speak with American accents, and this is quite acceptable to all.

A notable exception to the general rule is the cult of a black statue of the Virgin in a village called Siparia, a predominantly East Indian area in Trinidad. This is one of the most popular places of pilgrimage in the country, for Hindus as much as for Christians. It is a genuine example of a religious festival that has come from the people. So too there is the cult of St. Martin de Porres, the black Dominican brother who lived in Peru in the 17th century. St. Martin is a very popular saint in the region. A hymn sung in his honor has the verse:

> Race and station, pigmentation;
> They mean nothing to you, Martin
> To you all men are God's children.

The words bear witness to the racial implications of having a saint like Martin.

Another area where local symbols were not accepted by the churches is that of music. "Sacred music" means the same in the region as it does in Europe or North America. The fact that the drum is able to stir up deep spiritual sentiments in the hearts of the vast majority of people, especially those of African origin, makes no difference. Until recently it was totally unacceptable in a Christian church. Indian music, similarly, though deeply loved by the Indians in the region, is not heard at Christian services. Examples can be multiplied at will.

The same principle can be observed in the ethical teaching of the churches, for example in the area of marriage. The people of the region, especially those of African descent, have unique family patterns, the result of their history. In many areas it is rare for couples to get married in church and live in stable unions; the illegitimacy rate may be up to 80%. Yet the religious language of the churches in these places just would not reflect this situation. The content of the sermons, the prayers, the ideals presented would be little different from a culture where the nuclear family is the norm.

In short, the religious faith of the people is expressed in categories that are divorced from their everyday lives.

The free churches have had different emphases. They have given plenty of scope for the kind of religious experience that people of the region yearn for.

Here is the testimony from one of our West Indian writers:

> I was the only one in my village who belonged to the Church of England. My mother, who was brought up in this Church, had recently started to attend the Church of the Nazarene because she felt its services were more like part of her life, more emotional, more exciting, more tragic and more happy.

On the other hand, these groups have played little part in whole areas of life of the country, for example, in the field of education. Also, many feel that the kind of religious experience they offer serves rather to deaden the people's awareness of their plight than to encourage them to better their condition.

All this variety of Christian faith and practice, together with the great limitations of each variety, has resulted in a remarkable compartmentalization of religion. Compartmentalization first in the sense that there are areas which are simply outside the province of religion. The girl who has a baby out of wedlock has no sense of having done something wrong, nor do any of those who live around her. But she remains a convinced adherent of her church which, formally at least, imputes guilt to her. So too many of the leaders of thought in the society in this century have been deeply religious men and women. But their religion has played little part in the development of their ideologies. Many of their ideals were in fact very Christian, ideals for justice for the oppressed, for racial equality and national identity, but in fact there was no working out of a theology that integrated their ideals with their faith; it is almost as if both things existed side by side in their consciousness.

There is another kind of compartmentalization too, peculiar to the churches themsleves. Each church plays its role and people get from the different churches what they need at different times. They go to a crusade to fulfil one need and attend Mass to fulfil another. The contemporary ecumenical stance of the churches has merely recognized this long-standing practice of many of their members. It is also a phenomenon among Hindus, as mentioned previously in connection with the cult of the Virgin Mary in Siparia. So too the Catholic Abbey of Mt. St. Benedict is a place of prayer for people of all religions.

Some new factors have arisen that are modifying the traditional religious faith of the region. There is the recent emergence of a pentecostal movement among Catholics. Catholics are introducing elements into the church's life that were proper to lower class Christians, doing things that were considered to be beneath their dignity, e.g. having crusades or healing services, or being immersed for baptism. Many people are reacting to these innovations with disappointment, almost as if they would prefer the church to maintain its traditional style so that they would know where they stood, and desire the peaceful coexistence of the past.

Another new factor is the awareness that many people have of the ambiguous position of Christianity with regard to many of the ills of the society. This is due to the unquestioning acceptance of foregoing models, as I have mentioned, but also to the fact that many of the churches have been heavily involved in education, and the education system of the country is now under attack. Many have reacted to this awareness with a violent rejection of Christianity. Trinidad poet Derek Walcott captures this mood in his poem "Laventille":

> ... The black, fawning verger
> his bow tie akimbo, grinning, the clown-gloved
> fashionable wear of those I deeply loved
> once, made me look on with hopelessness and rage
> at their new, apish habits, their excess
> and fear, the possessed, the self-possessed.

During the race riots that shook Trinidad in 1970 many churches were attacked and in the two most important churches in the island the statues were defaced and painted black.

This has been followed by another movement. Many convinced Christians, some of them priests or ministers, have made a definite move to integrate their new consciousness into the church's life. This holds out much promise for the future. The period of transition is painful since the majority are scared of what is happening. There seems no doubt, however, that the general thrust is in the direction of a real adaptation of Christianity to the cultural environment.

Ewa Morawska

The Poles in Europe and America

TO say that in the course of stormy historical events a total of about one-fourth of the Poles found themselves outside the boundaries of the mother-country would be a conservative estimate. As a result of recurrent upheavals in the fight for national independence as well as extreme economic poverty, nineteenth-century Poland, semi-feudal and politically divided by Russia, Prussia and Austria-Hungary, had been sending millions of its inhabitants abroad. After 1918, the mounting difficulties which accompanied the reconstruction of the newly liberated country caused another exodus of thousands of Poles. Then the tragic events of World War II and the subsequent takeover of the Eastern European nations by communists drew Polish masses away from the fatherland.

Even though Poles often settled in the most unexpected, remote places on earth, some regions attracted greater proportions of the immigrants: the United States in North America, Brazil and Argentina in South America, Australia and Western Europe (France, Germany and Great Britain). Without doubt, the world-wide Polish diaspora is a fascinating field for compartive sociological study. Unfortunately, because of the specific historical conditions of the Polish migration to particular countries, as well as the significant differences in the social-cultural characteristics of the recipient societies, a thorough discussion of the problem in a single paper is a practically impossible task.

For example, migration from the Prussian part of Poland to western Germany at the turn of the century had the character of an internal, originally seasonal population movement. This permitted Poles settling in the rapidly developing industrial centers of the Ruhr Valley to maintain close and frequent contacts with their friends and relatives back in the old country. Also, the traditionally fierce and directly anti-Polish policy of the German empire had a significant impact on strengthening and perpetuating nationalistic feelings among the immigrants. France, a historical ally and refuge for the Polish political emigrés during the nineteenth century, only began to receive larger numbers of the working-class migration from Poland in the Twenties. A decade later, the Polish colonies in the mining regions of northern France grew through the secondary influx of highly skilled, industrial Polish workers from western Germany who fled the increasing hostility of the Third Reich. Contrary to the situation in Germany, France had not developed any official policy toward these foreign settlers and did not interfere with the internal life of the Polish communities. Military and political events during and immediately after World War II led thousands of Poles from all socioeconomic strata to Great Britain. A great majority settled in London, which thus became a political as well as highly politicized center of the Polish government in exile. This, along with the exclusive character of the British social structure, has accounted for the long-lasting isolation of the Polish community in England. The biggest group of predominantly peasant Poles settled in the United States in the second half of the nineteenth century and at the beginning of ours and constituted a part of a great economic migration from the poverty-stricken Europe. The Polish community in the United States, widely dispersed throughout the urban-industrial centers of this large and diversified country, is participating in the dynamic process of integration of the young, multi-national society. For many decades, a strong assimilationist pressure on the part of the dominant Anglo-Saxon culture, has been shaping the character of immigrant acculturation in the United States. The Canadian Poles, however, came to a country where the power structure was ethnically divided. The presence of a strong French element in Canada made it impossible for the English stock to form any unified assimilation policy toward the immigrants.

Besides the specific characteristics, the complex adaptive processes in Polish communities in different countries also display certain general similarities. Practically everywhere, the Polish masses entered the host-societies at the lower industrial echelons of the socioeconomic structure and the great proportions settled together in closely-knit ethnic communities.* Everywhere, the successive generations of Polish immigrants have been gradually making their way up the economic ladder and into the social environment of the recipient countries. The process of acculturation resulted in the formation of a new ethnic category as well as a distinctive cultural reality: not Polish, but Polish-French, Polish-Canadian or Polish-American.*

*The members of Polish communities abroad refer to themselves as *Polonian* rather than *Polish*, in order to indicate the difference between things Polish and, say, Polish-American or Polish-British.

Neither the prolonged economic and educational disadvantages of the majority of Polish immigrants in Europe and America, nor the overtly hostile (Germany), assimilationist (the United States) or at most indifferent (France, Great Britain) official policies of the recipient countries were conducive to the development of ethnic studies within or without the Polonian communities. Only recently, the new emphasis on cultural pluralism, particularly in the United States, caused a rapid increase in ethnic research. Although continuing to develop, Polonian studies still remain at the introductory stage, far from the comparative level, and it is questions rather than answers that they formulate. This paper will attempt briefly to present the development of the Polish communities abroad and to review some of the current issues. Special attention will be paid to the most researched Polish-American group in the United States, with occasional illustrations of Polonian life in other countries.

Since the Reformation movement in the seventeenth century and particularly during the partition of Poland by Protestant Germany and Orthodox Russia, the connection between national identity and Catholicism has become deeply engrained in the Polish cultural heritage. The historically internalized attitude which equated the notions of "Polish" and "Catholic" was carried over by the immigrants traveling to the foreign lands. Upon settlement in the new world, Poles, like other groups, naturally clung to the old ways in an effort to reestablish a familiar environment. In the East European villages, the local parish served basic needs of the community: it provided religious fulfillment, transmitted the cultural tradition and bound people together in primary relations. The enormous Polish immigration to the United States included many clergy and soon many Polish parishes flourished throughout the country much like "the old primary communities, reorganized and concentrated" (Thomas and Znaniecki, 1918). In the foreign, often hostile environment, efforts to defend Polishness in church and schools occasionally found almost xenophobic expression and the Americanization attempts of the Catholic hierarchy and public officials were frequently compared to the Muscovite (or Prussian) denationalization of the Poles. The situation of Polish immigrants in nationally homogenous Germany was much more difficult. The official policy strongly promoted a forced Germanization through the native Catholic church and by preventing the Polonian communities from building their own parishes and educating their children in the Polish culture. In those places, however, where the Polish parishes were established, they functioned as true bastions of Polish national preservation, similar to those in the old country. In France, the number of Polish priests was insufficient to provide for all the Polonian centers, but in the mining areas most populated by Poles, the Polish church was always the nucleus of further community development. The historical accounts of French Polonia also indicate that the presence of the Polish parish in a particular city was often of primary importance for arriving immigrants (Janowska, 1960). Half a century after the massive overseas migration, the Polish immigrants in Great Britain repeated the traditional pattern of ethnic settlement: the Polish churches lay at the core of local communities (Zubrzycki, 1956).

In most of the immagrant countries, the parish-centered Polonian groups developed a complex internal structure, where, for an extended period of time, the Polish religious and cultural traditions have been preserved in relative isolation from external influences. This may have slowed down the immigrant acculturation to the larger societies (and indeed, in the United States and Canada as well as in France and Great Britain, the Poles have been known to be particularly resistant to assimilation), but at the same time eased it tremendously. In a dynamic dialectical process, the ethnic church has been perpetuating the group national identity, *simultaneously* serving as the acculturative linkage between the community members and the outside world. In the United States, Canada, France and Germany alike, it was usually the parochial leadership which organized and represented the group interests on the public forum, and, through the connection with the native Catholic *nolens volens* introduced the elements of the host culture. Parochial school education, even though primarily oriented towards the transmission of the Polish national culture, was also imperceptibly socializing children into the values of the recipient society. Last but not least, the Catholic religion, the most sincere expression of Polishness, at times also unified different ethnic groups of the same faith on common issues in the United States as well as in Canada. The Polish communities abroad, despite the efforts to maintain the national traditions, were nevertheless absorbing new patterns, with the passage of time thus acquiring distinctive, *bicultural* characteristics.

Although little has been done in current ethnic research on Polonia, the fragmentary findings that exist are most contradictory. Specifically, there is minimal, if any, agreement in the existing studies as to the actual modifications in the multiple functions of the Polonian Catholic parish, a traditional stronghold of the immigrant national culture. In the triple-denominational United States (Protestant, Catholic, Jewish), the issue of the possible transmutation of the ethnic distinctions into more general, religious ones, is also ardently discussed. Therefore, without offering unwarranted conclusions, we shall briefly review some of the research findings related to the religious-community life of the contemporary Polonians.

A number of sociological studies indicate the persistence of the ethnically unifying, *social-communal* function of the Polonian Catholic parishes in Canada (Turek, 1960; 1967), France (Zywirska, 1961), Germany (Pietrzak-Pawlowski, 1961), Great Britain (Zubrzycki, 1956) and the United States (Sanders and Morawska, 1975:IV). It is also frequently reported that while other elements of the ethnic heritage are gradually dissolving in the native-dominant or pluralistic environment, the "Polishness" remains preserved in the *subcultural traditions* of the Polish Catholic church. For example, some students of the Polish-American and Polish-French communities point to the inter-class and inter-generational maintenance of the ethnic religious customs such as "Sharing the Christmas Wafer," "Blessing the Easter Basket" or keeping the portraits of the popular Polish saints in the homes (Sands and Morawska, 1975:IV; Zywirska, 1961; 1965).

On the other hand, it is often argued by Americans that the present religious and cultural expression of ethnicity, limited to ethnic community boundaries, is a distinctively working-class phenomenon. The proponents of this theory point to the abandonment of the traditional, folk-religious practices among the Polonians of successive generations and those higher in the socioeconomic status who enter the social and cultural world of the larger society. Similarly, the residential dispersion of the American Poles, originally concentrated in the immigrant ghettos, presumably leads to a gradual decrease in Polish church attendance as well as in the observance of the ethnic religious traditions. Interestingly, however, some studies found many Polonians from the suburban areas traveling from a distance to the old Polish parish which often remains the only tie with the otherwise abandoned ethnic community. Yet the younger, second and third generation Polish-Americans apparently have different motivations for attending the ethnic church than those admitted by the immigrants. While the latter usually point to a sense of *national duty*, the former indicate simple-religious and/or *social-recreational* reasons. It is therefore probable that the Polish church in the United States, though it does preserve the ethnic heritage, is indeed becoming less exclusively national and more religious and social in character. The important sociocultural process accompanies this transition. The current studies of the Polonian communities in Europe and America almost unanimously report an increase in the rate of exogamous marriages, a natural result of advanced acculturation. A slow, intergenerational growth in the number of inter-religious marriages is noted in Canada, the United States and even among British Polonians, the latter still much isolated from the dominant, Protestant society. In such exogamous families, however, the Poles practically always retain their Catholic faith. In France as well as in multi-national countries such as Canada and the United States, it is the Catholics who constitute the "mating pool" for the majority of intermarrying Poles.

A number of American scholars argue that, as the ethnic parishes become denationalized and supraterritorial and as the immigrant offspring achieve middle-class status positions and intermarry, *ethnicity* takes on a modified, *religious* meaning without its particular national references. Because of the previously mentioned, historical tradition equating "Polishness" with "Catholicism," it is extremely difficult to disentangle these two components in the process of ethnic acculturation. Except for some studies which indicate a decrease of religiosity among the Polonians advancing in generational succession and on the socioeconomic ladder (Sanders and Morawska, 1975:IV; Malanowski, 1960), the Poles abroad are generally known for their high and steady church attendance, high enrollment in parochial schools, and, as pointed out before, their preference for the religious endogamy (Sanders and Morawska, 1975:IV; Zubrazycki, 1956; Zywirska, 1961). Is then their observance of Catholic faith, norms and practices an expression of "national residuals" or does it reflect a new, "religious ethnicity" which unifies people of different backgrounds and common denomination in one pluralist society?

It was not the function of this paper to come to conclusions on the numerous issues posed by the contemporary ethnic studies. Much more research is needed to achieve a concise picture of the complex processes which account for the acculturation of the immigrants to the host societies. Without doubt, the Polish group in Europe and America is in the greatest need of such an effort.

Bibliography

H. Janowska, "Polska emigracja zarobkowa we Francji w latach 1920–1936", *Problemy Polonii Zagranicznej* (1960), 29–51.–

———, "Polska emigracja w Westfalii i Nadrenii w latach 1918–1939", *Problemy Polonii Zagranicznej* (1966/67), 118– 129.

J. Malanowski, "Adaptacja Polakow w Danii", *Problemy Polonii Zagranicznej* (1960), 124–155.

K. Murzynowska, "Polacy w Zaglebiu Ruhry w latach 1890–1914", *Problemy Polonii Zagranicznej* (1961), 114–136.

K. Pietrzak-Pawlowski, "Polonia w NRF po II wojnie swiatowej", *Problemy Polonii Zagranicznej* (1961), 199–210.

I. Sanders and E. Morawska, *Polish-American Community Life: A Survey of Research* (The Community Sociology Monograph Series II), Boston 1975.

W. Thomas and F. Znaniecki, *The Polish Peasant in Europe and America*, 5 vols. (University of Chicago Press), Chicago 1918–1920.

V. Turek, "Emigracja Polska w Kanadzie", *Problemy Polonii Zagranicznej* (1960), 51–95.

———, *Poles in Manitoba* (Polish Alliance Press), Toronto 1967.

J. Zubrzycki, *Polish Immigrants in Britain* (Martinus Nijhoff), The Hague 1956.

M. Zywirska, "Emigracja polska we Francji w swietle badan francuskich," *Problemy Polonii Zagranicznej* (1961), 225–234.

———, "Stosunek do tradycji narodowych mlodego pololenia polskiej emigracji gornicznej we Francji." *Problemy Polonii Zagranicznej* (1965), 185–199.

Mary Durkin

The American Experience:
An Irish Catholic Perspective

THE primary focus of the American bicentennial celebration has been commemorative of the events which occurred at the time of the Revolutionary War. Although it is not unusual at the time of an anniversary to reflect on the beginnings of what is being celebrated, much of the meaning and richness of an experience is lost if other events within the experience are neglected. So, too, with the American experience. America became a nation as a result of the Revolutionary War, but the country can be understood today only if we consider other events which have occurred during the two centuries of our nation's history.

America is a nation of immigrants. Two-thirds of the present population of the country did not have ancestors living in the original colonies at the time of the Revolution. The immigrant experience is as important an ingredient in an understanding of the total American experience as are those events which occurred two hundred years ago.

The story of the influx of immigrants to America and their settlement in large ghetto areas where they engaged in alien religious and cultural practices has received considerable attention. An equally intriguing aspect of the American experience, which is only beginning to receive attention, is the manner in which the children and grandchildren of these immigrants have become full-fledged members of the American society while still retaining, in varying degrees, a sense of being products of some other culture.

My personal focus for understanding what it means to be an American grows out of the fact that my ancestors immigrated here from Ireland in the last half of the nineteenth centry. The implications of my Irish heritage are becoming increasingly apparent to me as I examine the American experience seeking to discover what the pluralism of that experience says to the theological endeavor. The realization that there are others who, like me, find that their identity as Americans is colored by the culture of their immigrant ancestors has made it apparent that the pluralism of the American experience is much broader than the religious pluralism which was assured by our founding fathers when they decided to disestablish religion.

The children and grandchildren of the immigrants have participated in the American experience while simultaneously contributing to the character of the experience. The theologian must consider the lives of these Americans in developing a theological vision which will reflect the implications of this character and be viable for the American situation.

Obviously, in such a short space I cannot do more than offer some beginning observations on what I have discovered as I have reflected on my own experience. This has been a starting point for me as I seek to understand the claim of Harold R. Isaacs that the evidence, not only in America, but on a global scale indicates that everyone lives in a House of Muumbi, that is that our "essential tribalism is so deeply rooted in the conditions of his existence that it will keep cropping out of whatever is laid over it."*

The first twenty-two years of my life were spent in an Irish Catholic neighborhood on the far west side of Chicago. One fact which stands out as I reflect back on these years is the deep sense of self-satisfaction and pride which surrounded my membership in that community. We were not as affluent as some of the neighboring communities, but we regarded their show of wealth as ostentatious and were not envious.

The majority of the people in my neighborhood were Catholic. Though there were a few Protestants living on my block all my friends during my early years were Catholic. It seems as though the Protestants in our community did not have children. I can recall only one "public" (a term we used to describe all children who did not attend the Catholic school) in the immediate vicinity of my home; and, since that person was a he, I had few dealings with him.

The only close contact I had with Protestants during my early childhood years came from a friendship my Mother had continued from her work years. One of her closest friends was a Swedish Lutheran, and through her family I was exposed to Protestants as real people in a way which was not possible in our neighborhood. I have vivid memories of our attendance at their weddings, confirmation parties, and funerals and their attendance at ours. In both instances extreme caution was exercised to avoid active participation in the other's service.

Back at the neighborhood level I have no recollection of any Protestant family which participated as actively in a Church community as did my

*H.R. Isaacs, *Idols of the Tribe* (New York: Harper & Row, 1975), p. 26.

Mother's friend. There were two Protestant churches in the area, one a strict Baptist group which attracted members from outside the community since it was located close to public transportation. A crisis occurred each summer when members of the church came door to door inviting us to attend their Bible school in a big circus tent. We were admonished by our priests that this was not allowed. We were quite curious about what went on inside the tent, and, I think, a bit frustrated that we were not allowed to participate. I recall one summer pastime consisted of standing across the street and mocking the children who did attend.

In addition to being a predominately Catholic community, our neighborhood was predominately Irish. I do not recall as deep an emphasis on the Irish dimension of our character as there was on the Catholic dimension. This is not to say that we tried to reject our Irish background. Rather it reflected an acknowledgement that almost everyone in the community could trace at least one ancestor back to the Emerald Isle. The names of my childhood friends—Kavanaugh, Rea, Buckley, Sammons, Devereux, Whelan, Hanley—attest to this. Being Irish meant wearing green on St. Patrick's Day (and being angry at some of the Italians who moved into the community when they deliberately wore orange), hearing periodic references to mysterious sounding places in Ireland where one or another grandparent had lived (though the grandparents were long dead when I arrived on the scene) and listening to a friend's Irish-born grandmother speak disparagingly of the grandfather who was our next door neighbor. He, it seemed, was from County Mayo and she was from County Clare. His unkempt appearance was a bad reflection on Ireland, but, of course, according to her, was to be expected from someone from Mayo. Since I understood that my ancestors were from Mayo I tended to side with the man next door in these discussions.

Being Irish also meant knowing that we were different from the Italians when they began to move into the neighborhood. We all spoke English, and many of them spoke only Italian. Also they were much more emotional than we. It also meant hearing comments about why some families were different, perhaps because the father was German and exacting or the mother was German and quite particular about her house. One of my best friends in my early school years had a Bohemian mother and a German Protestant father. Obviously they were different. She cooked many Bohemian dishes, which I liked, but which my Mother could not cook. The father was nice, but he never went to church.

Obviously being Irish meant much more to my parents, both children of immigrants, but for the most part what it meant was not articulated to me. We were Irish, most of our neighbors were Irish and most of my friends were Irish. We were satisfied with our situation in life and did not, within the confines of our community, experience an adverse reaction to our Irishness.

Closely interwoven with my memories of satisfaction with my situation are memories of two sacred spaces within my community. It is, to some degree, the presence of these two spaces that contributed to my sense of satisfaction.

The first was the parish plant which for the most of the years I lived in the community consisted of a school, a convent, a rectory and a basement church. This place was the physical witness to the strength of our Catholic faith. It did not constitute our faith. I disagree with those critics who maintain that participation in Sunday service was the sum total of our religious experience. A physical plant, such as ours, was a symbol, though probably unconscious, of the spirit of the community. When I think of the parish, I think of the buildings, but not of a church empty save for the Real Presence. I think of the activities that went on within the confines of the different parts of the buildings and of the influence those activities had on my life.

It was to this place that I went each day for eight years of school. It was to the basement church that I went each day for many more years to attend Mass. It was to that same basement church that we brought the remains of my Father for the comfort of the Church's blessing. It was to the parish hall that I went for piano recitals and graduation parties. That same hall was the scene of high school dances, youth club meetings and variety show practices. Since I attended an all-girl high school this was an important part of my teenage development. It was to the new church that I went on my wedding day, for the baptism of my first child and for the burial Mass for my mother. It was from the rectory and convent that some of the most influential people in my early years came forth to teach me, to comfort me and to sow the seeds for good feelings about Church.

The other sacred space was evidence of our patriotism and summed up our loyal support of the war effort. Together with our neighbors we did all the things that loyal Americans did during those years. In addition we had block clubs where we joined even our Protestant neighbors in extra efforts. An outgrowth of the block club was the block memorial and I recall all the planning that went into choosing the appropriate location for the flagpole and plaque. Dedication of the spot and continual care of it indicated our American spirit. It was not necessary for us to work any harder than anyone else because we were Catholic or Irish. We accepted the fact that we were Americans, and even though the country had rejected a Catholic for the presidency we had no doubts about our authenticity as Americans.

My move to high school and college did not bring on any great concern about either my Irishness or my place as a Catholic, since the high school and college I attended were conducted by American Irish sisters and most of the student body was of Irish descent. Yet I do not feel that my Catholic "ghetto" existence was anti-American. I disagree with those who claim that an upbringing which exposes you only to others of the same religious background is detrimental to you as an adult. I was able to adjust to the situation as a student at a Protestant divinity school although I had attended sixteen years of Catholic school and could honestly say I had never had a Protestant friend.

However, as I move into situations where I mix with large numbers of people who are of different ethnic origins I have become aware of what my sense of being Irish has meant to me, though this was unconsciously gained. As I recognize that many of the behavior patterns of family and social living that I take for granted are not accepted by my new friends I have come to understand what the friends of my youth and I had in common without ever being aware of it. I also realize that my brand of Catholic experience has a distinct Irish cast to it that is not shared by my friends of different heritage.

Increased emphasis on understanding what it means to be Irish is not an indication that I am disloyal to my American heritage. It is rather an attempt to understand what makes me me and makes me similar to certain others and unlike certain others. Since most of this was acquired in an unconscious manner I doubt I could just will my Irishness away. I could choose to ignore it, but that would be ignoring an important part of me. Also, ignoring it will not eliminate the fact that my ancestors came to America from Ireland and passed on certain traits of Irish behavior. They also passed on a special type of American heritage which combined the experiences of those who had been here before them with the struggles of immigrant life. Their efforts forged out a new idea of what it means to be an American.

Their experience of being American and the heritage they passed on to me reflects the possibility that human beings can have loyalties to more than one group, that for the many to become one does not necessarily demand that the many become the *same*. The American experience gives witness to the fact that diversity and group identity do not mitigate against a spirit of cooperation. Our Irish Catholic neighborhood was different from the Italian, Polish and black neighborhoods of Chicago. When our sense of security freed us to cooperate with others our diversity was healthy. When we overemphasized our need to be best to the detriment of others, our diversity manifested some demonic tendencies. The theologian must be aware of the possibilities for both good and bad in the experience of diversity.

Before a theologian advocates a vision of all humankind merging into a oneness with no diversity he or she should consider how dull such a oneness would be. Even the Lord did not demand that the Samaritan cease being a Samaritan in order to be a model of the Christian way. The theologian must also be aware of a need for a plurality of Christian lifestyles if Christianity is to be viable for the many group experiences which join together to form a nation such as America. Symbols from the Christian tradition which speak to people who come from an Irish neighborhood might be of little meaning in a Spanish speaking community, even when these people have moved away from a specific ethnic community.

In conclusion, I think an experience of my daughter, Eileen, reflects the experience of many Americans. Eileen is quite conscious of her ethnic heritage. She is the family historian, assiduously composing the family tree and attempting to garner all available information about ancestors and living relatives. She has developed a deep interest in Irish culture and this past spring travelled to Ireland. Her father's aunts and uncles welcomed this fifteen-year-old Yank "home" and were most eager that she enjoy her stay. A surprise awaited her in the questions the relatives asked concerning her impressions of their country. Did she like it? How would she compare it with America? Which did she like better? She has the Irish gift of never giving a direct answer to a controversial question, but inwardly she wondered how anyone could imagine that she might find someplace better than America. Her love of things Irish and of Ireland has increased as a result of her trip, but she has also developed a conscious awareness of how highly she prizes being an American. She does not experience any contradiction in her loyalty to America and her love of the country and traditions of her ancestors. She would love to go to Philadelphia this Fourth of July. She also hopes to make many trips back to the land of her ancestors. She is more aware of her House of Muumbi than I was at her age. We can learn from her experience.

Raymond Breton

Reflections on the
French Presence in Canada

THE situation of the French group in Canada varies enormously from one part of the country to the other. These variations are evident on the demographic plane and also on the plane of social organization. As these objective conditions vary, individual or collective experience will vary accordingly. Therefore one must speak not of a French presence but of the French *presences* in Canada.

To start with there is a quasi-societal or quasi-global presence. This is to be found in Quebec first and foremost but, admittedly to a lesser degree, it is also the Acadian and North Ontarian presence. There is also a presence divided "between two worlds," to be found in the intermediary zone of social organization that divides the two linguistic communities. Although this zone is more social than geographical, one may still pinpoint such intermediary presence in certain regions as for example in the national capital. Finally there is in Canada a minority French presence which, though not entirely akin to that of other ethnic minorities, has much in common with them on the level of experience.

1

The French presence is quasi-societal by virtue of the fact that individual and collective experience takes place within the bounds of a francophone institutional ensemble. Whether the institutions in question be political, educational, religious, legal, sanitary, or in some degree economic, social form and content are largely dictated by the cultural imperatives of the French group. The French presence in Canada is thus to be defined in terms of the culture, institutions, and history which are germane to that group. Or, to put

42

it differently, it is at the heart of such a group that the greater part of individual experience takes place.

In a quasi-societal community, experience is affected as much if not more by internal developments (social conflicts, cultural and institutional change) than by events arising from its relations with other groups.

Minority experience,* as we will see later, is that which takes place primarily within the compass of institutions controlled by the cultural and social imperatives of an alien community. Developments affecting the institutional complex of that community will be the main factors affecting the experience of a minority group.

One must therefore speak of Quebec's experience in relationship to itself and its own history. In point of fact, over the past thirty years and especially in the last fifteen, French experience has been taken up with a skeptical inquiry into collective identity and cultural roots, the challenging of established elites in the institutions that personify them, and the dismantling of traditional structures. The most striking feature of this experience, for a time at least, has been its negativism. As Claude Racine wrote: "This metamorphosis has brought with it the disappearance of the schemes, the systems, the structures which have informed the life and thought of the man of Quebec up to now, and has left him destitute since he hasn't yet managed to create any new ones" (1972:157). In the context of a society in transition individual experience is one of rootlessness, of a loss of continuity with the past, of isolation. Novels published recently in Quebec put their protagonists through these trials. "A number of critics . . . have described the moral climate of these contempory novels: isolation, angish, dispossession, self-hatred, despair, impotence, failure and suicide. In these novels people cannot communicate with one another . . ." (Rioux, 1964:149).

Racine notes that in several of these works "the family has disappeared, the parish as well . . . all types of roots are absent. Men coexist . . . but they are alone in a hostile and indifferent world . . . . There is no conflict or revolt because the malaise cannot be seized upon. Objective liberty is total . . . . But subjective liberty is bereft of meaning" (1972:159).

If a sense of discontinuity can make a man feel he has lost his bearings, it can also bring on revolt and a complete rejection of the past, its structures and values. Where the Church is concerned, and in view of its dominant role in Quebec society, rejection and revolt have been generally kindled by the crushing morality of her traditional doctrine and its applications, clerical control of important institituional sectors, and her connivance with conservative schemes and often with social oppression. There are critics who have remarked on the frequency with which the theme of revolt appears in contemporary Quebec literature (see, for example, Filiatrault, 1964).

The term *minority* is used in its sociological and not its quantitative sense.

Scholars of contemporary fiction have in fact brought to light two tendencies which are almost contradictory: an inclination to despair, impotence, and failure on the one hand, and a drift towards revolt, rejection, and defiance on the other. The meeting of the two is the most telling characteristic of the French presence today. In his study of Antonine Maillet's *La Sagouine*, Shek has also noted these two currents: in this work passivity, defeatism, and fatalism go hand in hand with defiance and the struggle for the defense of human rights (1975).

Obviously uprootedness or revolt, the fight for personal liberation or the search for identity will not be experienced by all members of society to the same degree as the characters of a novel. Nevertheless, when the literature of an era is full of certain themes it may be considered an index to the corresponding experiences within the society in question.

I mentioned earlier the preponderance of the negative element in this matter. But it is not the only one worthy of note. The transformation of a society implies more than a rejection of its past and the disruption of its institutions. There is also a positive side to it, as exemplified in the new religious, artistic, literary, political, and economic experiences of the past few years—all of them valid on the individual as well as on the collective plane. The awareness of collective failure, the consciousness of a past clerical authoritarianism ruled by a morality which spelled the death of creativity can be a shaming thing; but the awareness of the potential inherent in a group, coupled with a realization that it has begun to relinquish the negative aspects of its tradition can, in the same measure, be a matter for pride. In spite of some misgivings as to the direction in which collective efforts are moving, the transformation of society through a "peaceful revolution" is acknowledged as something positive.

II

At the beginning of the last section I used the terms "quasi-societal" and "quasi-gobal." *Quasi* because the francophone institutional nexus is a broken one. Its economic base (finances, heavy industry, commerce) is to a great extent controlled by the members of another linguistic community. What we are dealing with, therefore, is an experience marked by feelings of insufficiency and subjection which have had their effect on the political and cultural planes.

The notion of belonging to a quasi-society, or a truncated one, is not resented as deeply when individual and collective life takes place in a rural or semiurban context. As Rioux has pointed out, the feelings of insufficiency and dependence first appeared with widescale urbanization and in particular with the coming of city life. "It is above all in the city that the Canadian learns of his subjugated, colonized condition; it is there that he discovers the economic and social alienation of his kith and kin . . . . Even if he has lived in a French quarter and attended French schools, he soon finds out that other people count more than he and his own when it comes to earning a living or scrambling up the social ladder" (Rioux, 1964:150). The change from a traditional to an urban, industrial society is for many the change from a society dominated by the clergy (in league with the petite bourgeoisie but unmolested by the English economic elite) to a society dominated by foreign economic interests (be they Anglo-Canadian or American). The sensation of uprootedness and feelings of revolt against moral constraints and the control of the clergy go hand in hand then with an awareness of the truncated nature of collective existence and a corresponding revolt against the other community.

I have already spoken of the evident alternation between feelings of defeatism and defiance, an alternation that may affect a person's relations with others or his own self-regard at different points in his life. Here once more a pendulum effect obtains: at times he will resent the burden of his own historical and cultural past and especially the domination of the clergy; at times he will resent the way anglophones control the economic resources of a society which is, in fact, deprived of the means for its own development. It is a swing that is not unrelated to the alternation of humiliation and pride we have already alluded to.

As the people of Quebec examine their collective problems, their economic and social condition, their backwardness in comparison with certain Anglo-Canadian circles, they inevitably ask themselves: "Whose fault is it? Who is to blame?" Anglo-Canadians have told them time and again that their culture is unsuited to an industrial world, that they live in *a priest-ridden society*, that they attach too much importance to family life and religion. For a long time now there have been a number of Quebec thinkers who have come round to this view. Latouche states that "the theme of collective guilt is nothing new in the mainstream of political literature in French Canada. It was dealt with successfully by Etienne Parent in the nineteenth century and Errol Bouchette at the beginning of the twentieth. In 1936 Canon Lionel Groulx was writing: 'What about responsibility? Who are the responsible ones? To which I would answer: all of us in fact . . .' Or (as Jean Pellerin wrote in 1963) it will not do at all to think that 'the English' are to blame for this exercise in political self-annihilation. One must at least give French Canadians credit for their own stupidity" (1970:565–66).

But if the question "Who is to blame" is answered in this manner, people will counter by bringing up the matter of English domination; of the collusion between the francophone political and clerical elite and anglophone economic interests with a view to maintaining, on the one hand, *a cheap labor pool* and on the other a servile, conformist community; of language discrimination; of exclusion from important posts in business and in commerce. In sum, the negative aspects of society will be attributed to its dependent status, to colonization.

On both the individual and collective planes, these two attitudes can be ambivalent. The burden of "one's own stupidity" lies heavy on each and every French Canadian's self-esteem. Even if he should manage to find some sort of explanation for it, he will not escape a certain measure of humiliation. It is in this context that he will turn against his own group and his own culture. But at the same time he will react against the dominance and discrimination that have brought him to his present condition and, to a certain extent, continue to keep him there.

On the collective level, one finds some thinkers and groups who put the blame on the community and its culture, and others who blame English domination and French dependence. Latouche (1970) tries to show that the "antiseparatists" or Federalists of Quebec have taken the first stance while the group in favor of independence supports the second.

This section on the experience of a truncated society cannot end without mention of the striking way in which the community has sought to assert itself and take charge of its own affairs in the past fifteen years. If I have chosen to dwell on the negative aspects of quasi-societal experience, it was in order to highlight the background against which these gestures of independence and self-affirmation have taken place.

III

In several regions of Canada, to be French implies a fragmentary and private experience: a minority experience. It is fragmentary insofar as it takes in some but not all aspects of existence, life as a whole being rooted in the institutions of the anglophone majority. What's more, this French presence implies above all private roles (in, for example, family life, religion, recreational activities) since the public ones (work, politics, consumer relations) are enacted in the context of anglophone institutions. Under these circumstances, the French presence in Canada hardly varies from that of other ethnic minorities.

But there is, nevertheless, one very important difference between the French and the other ethnic minorities which must be stressed in the light of its impact on the former. The francophone group thinks of itself as one of the founders of the Canadian nation. It stems from French migrants who not only came here, but who in fact came to forge a society. Indeed, with the exception of the Indians, their presence in Canadian territory antedates that of all other groups. And this means that the francophone minority is not an immigrant body pure and simple. The French Canadian's minority condition cannot be equated with that of immigrants who arrive to find a place for themselves in Canadian society. Its experience is rather that of a group which claims special recognition for its historical role.

But this desire for official recognition clashes with the demographic and structural realities of life for francophone groups, especially in the West of Canada. Representing a small percentage of the population and leading as they do a fragmentary and private existence, they are in no position to achieve special status. Their efforts in this direction in fact earn them more hostility than credit. On the other hand, their attempts at cultural and linguistic preservation are rather more acceptable since, on this level, they are only pursuing the same goals pursued by other minority groups.

Immigrants resent their own and their descendants' linguistic assimilation, considering it a greater menace than it really is. For them, linguistic assimilation is simply part and parcel of the "informal contract" they have entered into with the host society. This is not the case with the French Canadians, however, for whom it means defeat inasmuch as it contributes to their disappearance as a people.

The francophone community thus thinks of itself as a people with several centuries of life in Canadian territory; and yet in many parts of Canada the group which considers itself a people is structurally a minority. What we are faced with here is, then, an experience built out on structural contradictions.

In the light of all this, many individuals are ready to fall behind one of two options: either confine the minority status to Quebec, whose citizens are heirs to a historical process; or assimilate into the anglophone community so as to claim a larger share of a societal experience, even if it is not their own. The undecided, on the other hand, are doomed to a life of deep cultural insecurity, scarred by the contradiction of looking upon themselves as a people while leading the fragmentary and private existence of an ethnic minority.

References

Claude Racine, *L'Anticléricalism dans le Roman québecois (1940-1965)*. Montréal: Hurtubise HMH Ltée., 1972.

Jean Filiatrault, "Quelques manifestations de la révolte dans notre littérature romanesque récente," in F. Dumont and J.C. Falardeau (eds.), *Littérature et Société canadienne-françaises*. Québec: Presses de l'Université-Laval, 1964.

Marcel Rioux, "Alienation culturelle et roman canadien," in F. Dumont and J.C. Falardeau (eds.), *op. cit.*

Ben Z. Shek, "Thèmes et structures de la contestation dans 'La Sagouine' d'Antonine Maillet," *Voix et Images* 1 (décembre, 1975), 206-219.

Daniel Latouche, "Anti-séparatisme et messianisme au Québec depuis 1960," *Revue canadienne de Science politique* 3 (1970), 559-578.

Rogelio Duocastella Rosell

Internal Migrations
as Agents of Social Change

FEW people have remarked on the changes wrought by massive migrations in some parts of Europe today, and the impingement of these changes on the religious life of the entire population. Heretofore, scholars have focused on other aspects of the problem: the economic, with special reference to the effect of migrations on production and consumption; the educational, vis-à-vis the integration of children from a variety of cultures and speaking a variety of languages into the school system of the host country;[1] the matter of transport in summer and other holidays;[2] the availability and use of recreational facilities; the political issues, etc.

Where religion is concerned, although the pastoral side of the question has been explored to some extent, its sociological aspects have received less attention. Accordingly, the migrants' spiritual needs have been met by importing clergy and religious from their own homelands (which, in the event, are the most bountiful in priestly vocations),[3] rather than through a study of the problems posed by the clash of cultures and the attendant clash of religious outlooks.

Across Europe, given the variety of the immigrants' backgrounds, this "religious" problem has been of a multi-confessional nature: Muslims from Turkey and the Arab countries, members of the Orthodox Churches of Greece, Yugoslavia and other nations of the Southeast, Roman Catholics from Italy, Spain and Portugal have all set out for predominantly Protestant or Catholic regions. Simultaneously, the cultural problem assumes different proportions against the wide spectrum of European civilizations.

POINT OF REFERENCE

Our study refers to a specific area of the Continent, namely Catalonia, a zone which attracts heavy migrations from the most diverse regions of Spain. It deals, therefore, with an intranational problem, i.e., that posed by the influx of internal migrants.

Logically, if migrations give rise to a clash between different cultures superimposed on an international scale, when the superimposition occurs within a given nation the same conflict can obtain, although it may be less acute. In the former case, problems may arise as regards labor legislation, civil rights, administrative rulings, etc.; in the latter—the case under study—the difficulties will hinge on cultural factors such as lifestyle, language, customs, religious practices, consumer habits, social values, etc.

Before turning to the actual changes induced by these factors in the religious sphere, it would be well to quantify the demographic side of the problem and spell out the cultural differences between the various Spanish regions—for these differences are actually stronger than those that separate certain South American countries. In cultural terms, the principal groupings in Spain may be summed up as follows: *Catalonia* plus Valencia and the Balearic Islands, which together form a linguistic unit; *Castile,* including Old and New Castile, León and parts of Extremadura, which share a common language and history; *Galicia* and parts of Asturias, regions of Celtic origins and with a common tongue; the *Basque-Navarrese* region, sharing the same linguistic and anthropological backgrounds; and finally *Andalusia,* the last zone wrested from the Arabs, which is homogeneous in linguistic and ethnic terms.

The country's internal migrations have gone from its Southern and Central regions to Catalonia, the Basque Country and the capital city of Madrid. The bulk of the immigrants settling in Catalonia were Southern, though Castilian-Leonese groups came in their wake. Later still there were migrations from Galicia, but these were smaller in number. In demographic terms, the influx has been very high over the past twenty-five years. Indeed, in the two decades between 1950 and 1970, immigrants came to account for one fourth of the entire population:

Total population of Catalonia, 1950: 3,240,323 = 63%
Natural growth 1950-70: 691,958 = 13.5%
Migration, 1950-1970: 1,190,286 = 23.23%
Total population 1970: 5,122,567 = 100%

These migrations began in the decade between 1920 and 1930 and were halted in the years 1930-40, i.e., during the Fourth Republic and the Civil War. In the period 1950-75, Catalonia was to receive one and a half million immigrants—this in an area with an aggregate population of five and a half million. The migrant masses, mostly Andalusian and Castilian in origin, stemmed in their majority from rural milieus where regional and cultural ties ran very deep. Not only had these groups been isolated from one another across the centuries, but they had been roused to mutual antagonism, and confrontation, by the dire centralist policies of a Government whose mandate has always been defined in terms of stamping legislative, economic, linguistic and cultural uniformity on regions said to be agitating for separation.

THE PROCESS OF CULTURAL INTEGRATION

Some facets of this process have been analyzed by demographers and sociologists; the facts set out below have in effect been taken from studies carried out by the author and by the Institute of Applied Sociology and Psychology (ISPA) over the last fifteen years.

The present paper will refer, therefore, to some of the elements involved in any process of cultural integration. Indeed, it will consider religion as one of these elements, on a par with language, customs, values and lifestyles, so that it, too, will be seen as subject to integration, assimilation, adaptation and the other dynamics of social change.

The integrating process gets underway the very moment an immigrant arrives, and goes on for several years. In its first phases it is rather a process of "adaptation" to the local culture, followed by integration proper. Its mechanics have been studied up to a point, with the problems of language being perhaps the most favoured by scholars.[4]

Apropos of these problems it would be well to mention that, according to my own research in an industrial city in Catalonia in 1955, five years after their arrival 55% of the immigrants said they understood the language "perfectly." Among those who had been in the city between five and fifteen years, the figure rose to 78%, ultimately reaching 91% in the group which had spent even more time there.

But other, more interesting differences reflected their place of origin. Migrants from neighbouring regions with similar cultural traits scored 82% on the question of language. The rest naturally lagged behind but among them, too, local differences told, so that the results varied in accordance with their own regional backgrounds and their personal attitudes for or against adptation. Without going into the deeper motives of the phenomenon, suffice it to say that migrants from the South, who had perhaps come a longer distance than the rest, scored higher—67.9%—than those from Castile, who only reached the halfway mark of 51.6%.

One of the reasons for this disparity might be found in the vastly different socio-professional backgrounds of the two ethnic groups. The former, that is, the Southern migrants, were mostly construction or industrial workers; the latter were either members of the armed forces or civil servants. Other cultural factors such as fertility, birth rate, criminality, etc., were also studied and led to the same conclusion, viz., that in each case integration varied in strength and pace according to the culture of origin. Where fertility was concerned, although the migrants' index in their homelands had been very high (3.3%) compared to the host region (1.8%), adaptation was quicker than in other areas. But here, too, the pace varied according to the subjects' place of origin.

These differences in the pace and substance of integration seemed to us proof that the process was governed by restraints and impulses of a special type, mostly unconscious in nature, and conditioned by deep, strongly motivating complexes. When, in 1955, we set out to determine which of these complexes had the greatest bearing on cultural change, we found—and later confirmed—that perhaps the most important was that relating to *social prestige*. Interpretations of the "ruler/subject," "master/servant," "employer/ employee" relation, along with postulates regarding "esteemed/scorned occupation," "higher/lower social class," "residence in rich/poor neighborhoods," all combined to influence the newcomers' behavior.

Our study at that time was concerned with the mechanics of social mobility, a phenomenon made possible by the fact that the host population offered no resistance to the rise of the immigrants—in sharp contrast to the situation that prevailed in their homelands, where the lower classes were virtually condemned to labor at the same jobs generation after generation.

This access to a higher class and the possibility of reaching the standards of the host society, in turn produced a sharp reduction in the fertility and birth rate, the rapid acquisition of the local language, etc. What was afoot, therefore, was a process of adaptation-assimilation, but with a difference: it implied the reversal of a historical trend and the emergence of a paradox. The image of the country traditionally promoted abroad was that of the immigrants' Spain, not the Spain of the Catalans. Now, people whose way of life not only bore the official seal of approval but had become synonymous with the nation's, were themselves adapting to a "regional" culture.

THE SOCIOLOGY OF THE PURELY RELIGIOUS QUESTION

From the above remarks it would follow that a sociological study of the religious question should reveal similar differences, in keeping with the regional background of the immigrants and the nature of their overt religious observances. Unfortunately, analyses of the religious behavior and the quality of religious life in the different regions of Spain are so few that we have no valid basis for comparison. Nor has any exacting study been undertaken as regards the immigrants' religious practices in their own homelands. All we have to go by, then, are a few sociological premises derived from our own research and that undertaken by ISPA in the last few years. Of these, we would single out the following:

1. *The social value of the religious act.* The changes undergone by religious acts in the process of migration will vary in accordance with their inherent social content or value—proving thereby how much the immigrants' faith was dependent on local mores. When an act has deep roots in local folklore and tradition, and is spectacular in the bargain—e.g., the Holy Week processions of Andalusia—it will suffer considerably. For one thing, the new social and geographical ambiance is so different that it cannot complement or enhance the performance as the original setting did. Besides, the performers are now bound up with a different culture and, in the new urban setting, deprived of the social roles they played in their native communities. Furthermore, the new society spurns alien religious observances.

On a lesser scale the same thing happens with other religious practices. Attendance at Sunday Mass, for example, owes less to canonical precepts than to the pull of local customs and the sway of local sanctions on peasants who had never been adequately evangelized to begin with, and in such matters had simply clung to village tradition.

2. *The relative immunity of more personalized religious acts.* In contrast to the above finding, religious acts less bound up with the local ambiance, and therefore less "socialized," do not suffer as much from the upheavals of rural-urban migration. Based on the empirical data obtained—these acts are external and measurable—it can be categorically stated that the more intimate the religious observances, the more they are likely to survive. This applies to the whole gamut of such acts, from family devotions (common prayer, vows, solemn promises made for the recovery of the sick, etc.) to personal piety. Actually, all external religious acts are socialized to a greater or lesser degree, depending on their links with the wider milieu of the town or village or the intimacy of the family circle; and in effect, the moment they attach themselves to a concrete social ambiance, the ambiance will fix them, sustain them and preserve them. This is the principle which has forged the religious life of the immigrants, especially of those from villages in the rural districts of Southern or Central Spain, where the degree of socialization is very high.

3. *The influence of social prestige.* Another important factor in the inducement of religious change is the prestige attaching to the act in question or to the actors who take part in it. Every religious act is charged with social prestige or discredit; this is what determines much of its hold on the immigrant masses. The prestige factor will at times inhibit them from joining the ranks of those who perform it, as in the case of the poor woman who lives in a rich neighborhood and who was dismayed at the thought of attending Mass with well-to-do and smartly dressed people. By the same token, especially today, intellectual youths who feel going to Mass is *depassé* or unseemly for a modern and progressive young person, will also stay away. Inversely, the prestige inherent in the religious act can attract others, as, for example, the non-practicants who are drawn to Sunday Mass because it is

attended by members of the most socially prominent groups of the community. This is our explanation for the differentiated, and positive, behavior of immigrants in Vitoria, a city in the Basque Country where the index of attendance at Mass is considerably higher than that prevalent in their native towns or villages.[1] Likewise, the rise in Sunday attendance among the natives of a tourist zone in the Costa Brava in the Sixties was inspired by the religious habits of Belgian, Dutch and German tourists who spent the summer there: so great was the townspeople's urge to emulate them and court prestige that they, too, began to flock to Sunday Mass.

This craving for "prestige" also accounts for the wedding, baptismal and first communion celebrations favored by the poor in their eagerness to follow, as closely as possible, the behavior of the upper classes. Nor should we overlook the working class urge to enter children in schools run by religious (which were beyond the workers' means in the old days), at exactly the same historical juncture when parents of the upper classes, in Catalonia at least, are withdrawing theirs from such institutions for reasons no less sociological.

In our opinion the urge for "prestige" has and will continue to have great influence in the future. Indeed, we believe that on the religious plane, this craving has been more influential in shaping the immigrants' attitudes than their actual identification with a working-class ethos: class consciousness remains underdeveloped, though latent, among them. One would almost predict that in the near future, when the Spanish Church has managed a separation from the State and drawn closer to the people, working-class practicants will lapse as they begin to realize that allegiance to Catholicism (i.e., participation in its rites and religious observances) no longer betokens any social prestige.

3. *The role of urbanism in religious change.* Urbanism is another of the social factors which has a direct bearing on religious change among the migrants. An urban growth lacking in foresight and dictated solely by the economic ambitions of the upper classes has relegated the bulk of the immigrants to the outskirts of our cities. What we have in Spain is not a culturally-motivated exodus but a strictly socio-economic phenomenon. Our suburbs are not residential zones in the English style; they are simply outlying districts or patches of difficult terrain within the city (hillocks, shorelines, ravines, high ground) which the immigrants have made use of and where they set up their makeshift houses without too much difficulty.

The manner of their settlement —fast or slow, in ghettos far from the native population or at the heart of it (there being no discrimination whatsoever)—affects the course of the immigrants' integration.

Settlement in a city will affort them greater or lesser contact with the natives and the attendant possibility of absorbing the local culture, its values and religious attitudes. Thus the religious behavior of immigrants in rural towns in Catalonia and of those who have settled in large urban centers of the region is totally different. Religious and social integration is higher if the natives are encountered at work than if the contact takes place in the neighborhood or community. Curiously, immigrant women who do not go out to work had much greater difficulty in assimilating than their husbands, who had a chance to mix with local people at their places of employment. In the case of a city like Vitoria, where working-class circles are steeped in religious feeling, the immigrants' observance index was likely to rise rapidly. Then, too, along with this urban question and the influence of contacts with natives, one must reckon the matter of new sexual attitudes, i.e., the emergence of masculine piety, as this has also helped to raise the general observance index.

4. *The educational factor.* Yet another factor affecting the religious life of the immigrants is their level of instruction: orthodoxy rises in direct proportion to the education they may have received. Just as religious behavior varies in accordance with socio-professional standing (upper, middle and lower class métiers), so also will it reflect the subject's educational background. Those with little or no instruction are usually the ones with the lowest observance index while, inversely, the more educated individuals will practice more. Of course, the social and educational categories overlap to a great extent.

The most interesting point in this connection is the drop in the observance curve when higher studies are reached. Every survey undertaken among natives of Andalusia, the Levant and the central regions of the country, showed that the curve of religious practice rose consistently in accordance with the level of instruction up to and including the upper baccalauréat. Once it crossed the university threshold, it lost momentum. When the study was carried out among the immigrant population, the same thing happened. What is the explanation of this?

In our opinion the mechanics of social integration are as applicable here as on all other planes. When the immigrant reaches a higher level of personal independence and security, his efforts to integrate will decline accordingly. In other words, when he no longer feels himself beholden to the new ambiance, his greater security and self-sufficiency will make him relatively impervious to change. We have been a witness to this phenomenon as regards the language, culture and, by extension, the religious observances of the host community.

This finding also confirms the classic sociological conclusions that may be drawn from the religious behaviour of the two groups. People of high intellectual standing will go it alone, ideologically, with far more security, and will therefore feel freer to assert their own cultural and religious points of view. The majority of Spain's internal migrants, by contrast, are drawn from the country's least educated classes. Their religious observances are less rational and introspective, and more attuned to the world of the emotional and the cosmic; their external acts, on the other hand, are so highly socialized that the absence of the old constraints in a new ambiance will induce laxity more often than not.

CONCLUSION: CULTURAL, SOCIAL AND GENERATIONAL FACTORS IN THE RELIGIOUS SPHERE

In this article we have endeavored to throw light on the role of cultural elements in the inducement of religious change. To this end we have adduced a set of sociological premises applicable in Catalonia, a region of Europe where large migrations from zones with widely different cultures (notably Andalusia and Castile) raise unique internal problems.

We have seen the vulnerability of religious observances rooted in specific geographic and cultural milieus and, as such, highly socialized. We have noted the drastic change they undergo when they are borne on the tide of migrants drawn from the least educated and poorest groups, and the damage done, inevitably, by the social prestige or discredit attaching to these observances in the eyes of the upper classes in the host community.

But we should not end without mentioning two other factors which also bear directly on religious change: the questions of generation and of class (in the sense of social hierarchy). We came across them in a survey conducted among practicing Catholics in Catalonia, by means of which we measured religious behaviour, attitudes, values, motives and even simple opinions against a set of sociological criteria. In the course of this research it was found that:

1. The two leading variables in the socio-religious statistics for Catalonia (extensive perhaps to the Western world of which it forms part) were quite obviously those relative to generation and class. In each case the variance index was three times higher than that produced by the cultural (or geographic) measurement, and is proof that today the generational is the most telling factor where religious behavior, outlook, attitudes and motives are concerned.

2. Next in importance was the variable relating to social class. The fact of provenance from working, middle or upper class groups, with their respective socio-professional and economic characteristics, was found to have considerable influence on the individual's religious behavior, and a progressive effect on his religious opinions and rationales.

3. If both these factors proved more telling than the question of culture, or place of origin, the latter turned out to be twice more important than that of sex, heretofore considered almost decisive. In other words, the man/woman ratio was found to have less influence on the religious profile of the group and especially on its external manifestations—which, as we have seen, are subject to other factors.

These sociological findings can afford a wealth of pastoral insights. Followed up with due attention to the underlying anthropological problems, they could yield much valuable fruit.

Notes
1. See the efforts of the German Federal Republic through its Project Alfa.
2. Cf. the statistics published by the I.L.O.
3. In 1964, following a sociological study of tourism on the Costa Brava, the bishop of Gerona pressed into service foreign priests who ministered to the visitors during the summer. Other Spanish bishops have followed his lead.
4. Note that between Castilian and Catalan there are much the same phonetic and semantic differences as between Castilian and, for example, French and Portuguese.
5. We have found that immigrants from the same region (Andalusia) and the same milieu (rural), upon arriving in an industrial but fervently Catholic city in the north of Spain (Vitoria) increased their attendance at Sunday Mass fourfold (from 8% to 33%). Meanwhile, immigrants from the same Andalusian zone, upon settling in an industrial city in Catalonia where the index of Catholic practice was much lower (Mantaró), only produced an observance index of 11.5%.
6. Cf. R. Duocastella, Cambio social y religiosos en España (Barcelona: Editorial Fontanella, 1975).

Andrew M. Greeley

Editorial Summary

THE format of this issue, *Sociology and Religion*, is somewhat different. We present empirical data first of all—a series of articles with sociological evidence and commentary, or at least personal experiences. Then the present writer summarizes the sociological data and addresses certain questions to the theological writers. After their articles, Gregory Baum responds in a final editorial commentary. Unfortunately, it was simply not possible to have the sociological "input" articles available to the theological commentators before they wrote their essays. Hence the two editors had to anticipate what the authors of the articles in the first half of the issue would say when they assigned topics to the authors of articles to appear in the second half. The strategy seems to have been successful; a "correlation" does exist between the "existential situation" on the one hand and the "Christian illumination" on the other. The tangled complexities, the richness, the variety, and the dangers of ethnic diversity do indeed seem to be illuminated by the Christian symbols analyzed by Anderson, Murphy, Vawter, Shea, and Tracy.

It is possible at this stage in the rediscovery of ethnicity in the Western world to consider oneself dispensed from the need to remark how astonishing it is, in our supposedly universalistic, rationalistic, and achievement-oriented Western society, that "primordial ties" (Clifford Geertz) and "idols of the tribe" (Harold Isaacs) have survived. The first international conference on the subject, sponsored by the Ford Foundation and presided over by Daniel P. Moynihan and Nathan Glazer (reported in their book *Ethnicity*) is sufficient indication that the ethnic factor is important not only in such clearly ethnic pluralistic societies as the United States and Canada but also in such supposedly homogenized countries as France, Spain, Germany, and Great

Britain.

There are, however, three other themes that seem to run through the essays in the first section of this issue.

1. The attractiveness of the ethnic heritage. Deverteuil, Charles, and Harvey are proud of their Trinidadian culture. The Polish emigrants that Morawska describe are not ashamed of being Polish. Mary Durkin's daughter, Eileen, sees no conflict between being American and Irish and neither, for that matter, does her mother. There is surely little guilt among the Europeans described by the Connors in their pride of origin, and it is scarcely necessary to remark that the French Canadians are not ashamed of being French and Canadian. Furthermore, if one looks at the theological essays to follow, one will note that such sophisticated theologians as Tracy and Shea have strong sympathies for their own Irish cultural background. In other words, not only has ethnicity survived but it has survived even among the intelligentsia. Sophisticated scholars are not merely nostalgic about their own traditions; they are capable of seeing within those traditions elements that still have something important to contribute to the contemporary world. Ethnicity is doubtless a powerful force, and part of its power would seem to come from the pride one takes in the attractiveness of one's own ethnic tradition.

2. Ethnicity is a terribly ambivalent dimension of human life, as Harold Isaacs has observed. It enriches human culture but it also leads to violence and death—some twenty million people, according to the Hudson Institute, died in ethnic wars since 1945. There are tensions in Trinidad, French Canada, Northern Ireland, and the United States (to list counries directly treated in the preceding articles) which could explode at any time. Ethnically heterogeneous societies, be they small like Trinidad or large like the United States and the Soviet Union, survive only because those who preside over them are remarkably skilled in channeling ethnic dynamisms into constructive or at least harmless directions. Ethnicity is not only powerfully attractive but it is also potentially powerfully destructive.

3. It is finally clear that ethnic diversity is offensive. The English Canadians consider the French Canadians to be different and somewhat inferior. Many Americans consider the Polish immigrants and their children and grandchildren to be different and therefore inferior. Many of the whites who once dominated life in Trinidad are still convinced that the blacks, because they are different, are inferior. Ms. Durkin seems constrained to defend her Irish heritage against those Americans who insist that she must give it up. The price for acceptance by the dominant group in a society, in other words, is often the abandonment of one's own heritage. "Why can't *they* be like *us*?" is, if not a universal human question, at least a universal human temptation. That which is different is suspicious, inferior, and quite possibly dangerous. We must get them before they get us.

Homogenization does not in principle seem to be an unrealistic demand. If you want to be a Canadian, become a good Englishman; if you want to be an American, become a good Anglo-Saxon; if you want to be a Trinidadian, become a good white (at least culturally). How can one have a united society, in other words, unless one has a common culture from which the potentially divisive particularisms have been eliminated? It seems a reasonable question.

However, as soon as the question is raised, its absurdity is seen. Why should I become like you? Why shouldn't you become like me? What is there about your heritage that makes it superior to mine? Why can't I be an American and Irish, Canadian and French, or Trinidadian and Indian? Why should I make the sacrifice and not you? Because you are richer, more powerful, or were here first? I'm sorry, but that won't work.

The appeal to universalism, then, while seemingly reasonable, flies in the face of the fundamental human truth that we are the products of our own pasts and those pasts are different. Unity is achieved in human societies not by homogenization but by the integration of diversity; and the potential for conflict inherent in diversity is not minimized by either ignoring it or eliminating it but by facilitating pluralistic integration. Homogenization may be neat, simple, and theoretically easy while pluralistic integration is difficult, complex, messy, confusing, and an endless threat to people who like their world simple. However, despite all the moralistic, self-righteous philosophical statements about the necessity of deemphasizing that which is different among us, human beings do not seem disposed to follow such advice. Pluralistic integration of diversity is not merely an alternative to homogenization, it is in fact the only effective response to the fundamental datum of human diversity. We live together as different persons not by eliminating our differences, not by denying them, not by fighting over them but by learning to tolerate them, respect them, and perhaps even to enjoy them.

The late Lloyd Fallers—one of the few saints I have known in my life—used to attend our seminars in pluralism at the National Opinion Research Center. He once remarked to me that it was interesting to notice how much laughter there was at the seminars. "Did you ever ask yourself why everybody laughs so much?" he said one day. I made some foolish comment about it having something to do with my own sense of humor. Tom (as we called him) smiled. "Well, it may be that, too; but you see, in your seminar staff and students are discussing something that is extremely important to their lives, something that is very intimate to them, something that they reverence and respect. Either they laugh over the differences that exist in the room to ease the tension or they fight over them. Ethnicity is not something neutral; it is either enjoyed and laughed at or you fight about it."

It is to be assumed that the Lord God, who created with reckless disregard for simplicity, had his own reasons for making his creation diverse. It now seems appropriate to turn to our theological colleagues and ask the question, "How come?"

PART II

Theological Response

Bernhard Anderson

The Babel Story:
Paradigm of Human Unity and Diversity

THE story of the building of Babel/Babylon (Gen. 11:1-9) is important for a theology that considers, on the one hand, our common humanity as creatures of God and, on the other, the manifold pluralism in the Creator's purpose. The story portrays a clash of human and divine wills, a conflict of centripetal and centrifugal forces. Surprisingly, it is human beings who strive to maintain a primeval unity, based on one language, a central living-space, and a single aim. It is God who counteracts the movement toward a center with a centrifugal force that disperses them into linguistic, spatial, and ethnic diversity.

The Babel story reflects the concrete realities of ancient Mesopotamia, a cradle of civilization. It includes true-to-life details which accord with archaeological knowledge, such as the use of kiln-fired bricks to compensate for the lack of natural stone in the Mesopotamian plain, and the construction of tiered temple-towers, like the famed ziggurat of Babylon known as Etemenanki. These archaeological details, however, are ingredients of an artistic portrayal that transcends the ancient cultural setting and hence becomes a paradigm of human life in all times and places. Accordingly, the story stands at the climax of the *Urgeschichte* (Gen. 1-11) whose meaning and scope are universal. The element *Ur-* refers not only to what lies in the distant, mythical past (primeval) but to what is constitutive of history itself (primal).

Often the narrative has been regarded as a story of tragic failure, of the loss of the unity that God intended for his creation. The assignment to write this essay was accompanied by the editors' reminder that in the Middle Ages scholastic theologians understood the story to mean that ethnic pluralism was largely the unfortunate result of human sinfulness. In one way or another this negative view has survived in Christian circles to the present day. For instance, Jacques Ellul, a layman of the French Reformed Church, insists in his provocative work, *The Meaning of the City*, that the story is a paradigm of Man's declaration of independence from God and that it is essentially related to the story of the Fall. The city, he maintains, is the locus of evil in human history and is "the great enemy of the church."[1] There is a measure of truth in these negative interpretations, but they are one-sided and not sufficiently contextual. For one thing, in the larger perspective of the *Urgeschichte* the diffusion and diversification of humankind clearly is God's positive intention. In the beginning, God lavished diversity upon his creation; and his creative blessing, renewed after the Flood, resulted in ethnic pluralism (Gen. 10). Furthermore, eschatological portrayals of the consummation of God's historical purpose do not envision a homogenized humanity but human unity in diversity. According to the Isaianic vision (Isa. 2:1-4), when the peoples in the last days stream to Zion, the City *par excellence*, they will come as nations with their respective ethnic identities. And when the Spirit was given at Pentecost, according to the New Testament account (Acts 2), human beings "from every nation under heaven" heard the gospel, each "in his own native language," in the city of Jerusalem.

The Babel story contains a peculiar dialectic. Man strives to maintain unity, God's action effects diversity. Man seeks for a center, God counters with dispersion. How are we to understand these centripetal and centrifugal tendencies? I propose to reexamine this question by considering, first, the Babel story as a discrete narrative unit and, second, by considering how this pericope functions in the context of the *Urgeschichte*. In the end, having seen the part in relation to the whole, we may be able to understand how the story illumines a theology of pluralism.

Considered by itself, the Babel story is a masterpiece of narrative art. In very brief compass and with an amazing economy of words, the narrator has produced a symmetrical literary structure which is well-rounded and complete. The independence of the pericope is indicated, on the one hand, by its dissonance with the previous Table of Nations (ch. 10) in which linguistic, territorial, and ethnic diversity is already realized and, on the other, by the ensuing Shemite genealogy (11:10-26) which clearly belongs to a different literary genre.

Here it is not possible to consider the various stylistic features which show that the story is an inspired literary work of art, like a poem. For our immediate purpose, it is noteworthy that the story occurs in two movements which balance each other. In the first part (vss. 2-4, after the introductory line), human beings are the actors. In the course of their nomadic wanderings from an undesignated source, they came upon a plain in "the land of Shinar," or Babylonia (cf. 10:10), and there they settled down. Determining to make their settlement permanent and to preserve their family-like unity of language, they worked with energy and resourcefulness, as indicated by the twofold resolution, "Come let us . . ." Their ability to make artificial stone (kiln-fired bricks) was a creative accomplishment; and this technological breakthrough spurred them to build a city, whose distinctive feature was an impressively high tower. If we assume that the tower was a ziggurat, and not just a military fortress, they were apparently a religious people, not unlike Christians who down through the centuries have built in the center of their cities a cathedral with a lofty spire.

In the second part (vss. 5-8), Yahweh is the actor. From his heavenly abode he "came down" to examine the ant-like enterprise of human beings, ridiculously microscopic from a cosmic perspective; and he realized that, having begun so well, nothing was to prevent them from completing their task and even undertaking more ambitious projects. So, in language that echoes that of the resolute builders ("Come, let us . . ."), he intervened, not by causing the tower to topple on the people but by confusing their language so that there was a failure of communication. The result was that Yahweh dispersed them from their chosen center, and they had to stop building the city.

The story concludes with an ironic twist (vs. 9). Those who wanted to make a name for themselves received a memorial, but it was a name of shame. Here Babel does not mean "gate of the god(s)," as in Akkadian where the term suggests that the temple center was the omphalos where heaven and earth meet and where human beings experience contact with the Divine; rather, by a Hebrew word-play Babel is understood to mean "confusion" (*balal* = "confuse, confound"). Moreover, the people who wanted to settle securely "there" (vs. 2), in one metropolitan and religious center, were scattered "from there" over the face of the earth (vs. 9). Thus the ending recapitulates the beginning, though by way of a reversal.

What motivated the actors in the drama? On this question the text is ambiguous. Apparently the builders transgressed, but this is not stated outright, nor is their sin specified. And apparently Yahweh was worried about what human success might lead to (vs. 6; cf. 3:21!), but no reason for his intervention is given. The narrator does not attempt to fill in the gaps prosaically, leaving nothing to the imagination; rather, the hearer is invited into the story's dimension of depth and mystery. Here it is appropriate to recall Erich Auerbach's discussion, at the beginning of his *Mimesis*, where he contrasts the style of the Homeric story of Odysseus' Scar ("uninvolved and uninvolving") with that of Gen. 22 (The Testing of Abraham), which calls upon the reader to enter the story and fill in the gaps.

Since the Babel story is fraught with ambiguity and has various levels of meaning, it is not surprising that interpretations vary. Christian expositors tend to favor a maximum interpretation: the human beings were motivated by a Promethean impulse to storm the heavens and to be like God. Thus, the story portrays human hybris and divine nemesis.[2] On the other hand, a line of Jewish interpreters, beginning with Josephus (*Ant.* I, iv, 1), advocates a more modest view: the builders' intention was to gather the people into a centralized location and thus to resist God's purpose that they should multiply, fill the earth, and subdue it.[3] According to this interpretation, the description of the tower "with its top in the heavens" means nothing more than an impressively high structure such as the Canaanites built (Deut. 1:28; 9:1)—a skyscraper in modern terms.

The motivation is indicated in balancing positive and negative terms (vs. 4b): "Let us make a name for ourselves, lest we be scattered over the face of the earth." Westermann finds in this mixture of motives evidence that the story has undergone a traditio-historical growth. Originally the human resolve (vs. 4a) was simply "an expression of a will to greatness, a will to excel" ("Ausdruck des Willens zur Grösse, zum 'Überragenden' ");the motive of fear of being scattered was a later expansion.[4] If, however, attention is given to the stylistic unity and symmetry of the story, one sees clearly that the theme of "scattering" is intrinsic to it, occurring three times at strategic places: the first part (vs. 4b), the second (vs. 8), and the conclusion (vs. 9). The positive and negative aspects of the motivation—making a name and fear of dispersion—belong essentially to the paradigmatic portrayal of the human situation.

Strikingly, the people are described as acting in democratic concert: "Come, let us . . ." There is no suggestion that the project was under the leadership of a king, like those Babylonian rulers who engaged in architectural works to make a name, as we know from ancient royal inscriptions. The motivation was deeply human. To be sure, the builders sought material glory and fame; but more than this, they sought dominion over the limitations of their environment. Animals are gregarious, but they do not build cities. The city is the symbol of Man's creative freedom to rise above his natural environment and to come together in social unity. It is a place of security from powers of chaos that threaten from the outside world. It is a place where people may raise a memorial, even a religious monument (a ziggurat or a cathedral) which, at least for a period, stands above the flux and contingency of history. Yet human freedom displays an ambivalent mixture of creativity and anxiety, and therefore the words "lest we be scattered" are appropriately joined with the "name" which signifies dominion. The Jewish scholar, Jacob, rightly stresses the anxiety that accompanies human aspiration and gregariousness. The builders, he says, "do not want to force their way into the heavens, but to huddle closely together on the earth where they fear getting lost."[5] Fear of the unknown—the trackless wilderness, strange places and faces, the uncertainties of the future—may impel a nomadic people toward a center, where they organize to build a city. The builders may even surrender their primitive democracy to an aggressive leader like Nimrod who promises political security and imperial renown. But this goes beyond our story, although Nimrod was also associated with Babel according to another tradition (10:8-12).

There is something very human, then, in this portrayal of people who, with mixed pride and anxiety, tried to preserve primeval unity. However, their intention to hold on to the simplicity of the past collided with the purpose of God who acted to disperse them from their chosen center.

Let us proceed to another matter. The Babel story now functions in a larger narrative context which enhances its meaning. It is generally recognized that the story is the climactic episode of the old Epic tradition (the Yahwist Epic or J) which portrayed world history from the creation to the call of Abraham. It is also important, however, to consider that the final redactor of the Pentateuch, the Priestly Writer, has incorporated large portions of this old Epic into his work for the sake of enrichment and elaboration. Therefore, the interpreter must take seriously the final form of the tradition and, in this case, the ethnological framework within which the Babel story functions.

The story comes immediately after the so-called Table of Nations (ch. 10). There is an obvious seam between these two traditions. The Babel story begins with the assertion that people spoke the same language; the Table of Nations, however, indicates that already the family of Noah had proliferated into a multitude of ethnic groups. How are we to understand this dissonance?

Some light is thrown on this question by studying the editorial method used in appropriating blocks of old Epic tradition. The redactor gives primacy to his own priestly material; but at appropriate places he adds old Epic tradition which harks back to an earlier point in the priestly outline and, to a certain extent, is parallel. For example, he begins with the priestly creation story (1:1-2:3); then, after his toledoth ("generations") formula (2:4a), he adds a block of Epic material (2:4b—4:26) which at the outset duplicates and parallels the priestly account of the creation of Man, male and female. Also, in ch. 5 he presents the toledoth of Adam up to the birth of Noah's sons; then he introduces a block of Epic material (6:1-7:8) which, at its beginning, reaches back to an earlier, indefinite point in time. After the Flood Story,[6] he continues with the basically priestly Table of Nations; then he adds the Babel story which reverts to an earlier time before the proliferation of Noah's sons into ethnic and linguistic groups. In proceeding thus, the redactor attempted to preserve the traditions and, at the same time, to enrich and fill out his own outline. In the specific case of the Babel story, he may have thought that this episode provided an etiology of the ethnic pluralism of ch. 10. Be that as it may, the story is supplemental. It adds a dimension that is necessary for a full understanding of the interaction of divine and human purposes in the *Urgeschichte*. The late Old Testament theologian, Gerhard von Rad, rightly observed—though without pursuing fully the implications of his remark—that "the chapters must be read together, because they are intentionally placed next to each other in spite of their antagonism."[7]

The redactor's intention is evident primarily in the way he combined materials which once had an independent meaning, with the result that the whole is greater than the sum of the parts. It is noteworthy that, when dealing with the post-diluvian period, he displayed a special interest in the "scattering" motif, thrice repeated in the Old Epic Babel story. In a transitional passage (9:18-19), it is stated that the whole earth was "peopled" (literally, "was scattered") from the sons of Noah. This theme is reiterated in the Table of Nations: in 10:18 where the same verb is used of the "spreading out" of the Canaanites, and especially in the Priestly Writer's summary sentence in 10:32 where he uses a synonymous verb: "These are the families of the sons of Noah, according to their genealogies, by their nations, and from these the nations *branched out* after the Flood." In these instances, ethnic diversity is understood to be the fruit of the divine blessing given at the creation and renewed in the new creation after the Flood (9:1, 7; cf. 1:28). From the "one" (Noah) God brought into being "the many" through the ordinary course of human increase and population expansion.

How, then, are we to understand the juxtaposition of two traditions: one which perceives that God's blessing is manifest in manifold diversity, and the other which suggests that God's judgment is disclosed by his dispersal of human beings from a center?

One thing is clear: when the Babel story is read in its literary context there is no basis for the negative view that pluralism is God's judgment upon human sinfulness. Diversity is not a condemnation. Long ago Calvin perceived this truth. Commenting on Gen. 11:8 ("So the Lord scattered them abroad"), he observed: "Men had already been spread abroad; and this ought not to be regarded as a punishment, seeing it rather flowed from the benediction and grace of God." He continued: "But those whom the Lord had before distributed with honour in various abodes, he now ignominiously scatters, driving them hither and thither like the members of a lacerated body."[8] No longer is it necessary, however, to try to harmonize what "Moses" wrote. There are tensions and dissonances in Scripture which have arisen during a long history of traditions, from the early oral period to the final composition of the Priestly edition of the Pentateuch during the Exile. The Priestly Writer/Editor has given us a final composition in which his presentation of the *Urgeschichte*, based on a genealogical scheme, is enriched with old Epic tradition.

Viewed in this light, the Babel story has profound significance for a biblical theology of pluralism. First of all, God's will for his creation is diversity rather than homogeneity. Ethnic pluralism is to be welcomed as a divine blessing, just as we should rejoice in the rich variety of the non-human creation: trees, plants, birds, fish, animals, heavenly bodies. The whole creation bears witness to the extravagant generosity of the Creator. But something more must be added, and this the redactor has done by supplementing his work with the old Epic story of the building of Babel. Human beings strive for unity and fear diversity. They want to be securely settled and are fearful of insecurity. Perhaps they do not pit themselves against God in Promethean defiance, at least consciously; but even in their secularity they are driven, like the builders of Babel, by a creative desire for material glory and fame and a corresponding fear of becoming restless, rootless wanderers.

This creative freedom is both the grandeur and the misery of Man. On the one hand, it enables human beings to rise above the limitations of their environment and, with cooperative effort and technological ingenuity, to build a city which affords unity and protection. On the other hand, their "will to greatness," which also reflects anxiety, prompts an assertion of power which stands under the judgment of God.

Human beings are, indeed, "members of a lacerated body"—a broken, fragmented society in which God's will for unity in diversity is transformed into conflicting division between peoples who speak different languages, live in separate territories, and belong to particular ethnic groups or nations. The *Urgeschichte,* however, leads beyond the Babel story toward the call of Abraham. Uprooted from his Mesopotamian homeland and moving by faith into the unknown, he is a paradigm of a new people through whom all the families of humankind are to experience blessing, not by surrendering their ethnic identities, but by being embraced within the saving purpose of the God who rejoices in the diversity of his creation (cf. Rev. 7:9-12).

Notes

1. Trans. from the French by Dennis Pardee (Grand Rapids, Mich.: Eerdmans, 1970). See pp. 10-20.

2. This view is recently advocated on the basis of stylistic criticism by J.P. Fokkelman, *Narrative Art in Genesis*, Studia Semitica Neerlandica (Amsterdam: Van Gorcum, 1975), pp. 11-45. However, Donald E. Gowan, in *When Man Becomes God: Humanism and Hybris in the Old Testament* (Pittsburgh: Pickwick Press, 1975), concludes that in the Babel story the hybris motif is present only "in a subdued form" (pp. 25-29).

3. This interpretation is given in the Genesis commentaries by Benno Jacob (1934) and Umberto Cassuto (1949); also in Nahum Sarna, *Understanding Genesis* (New York: McGraw Hill, 1966), pp. 63-77.

4. Claus Westermann, *Genesis,* Biblischer Kommentar, I (Neukirchen-Vluyn: Neukirchener Verlag, 1974), p. 727.

5. Benno Jacob, *Das erste Buch der Torah: Genesis* (Berlin: Schocken Verlag, 1934), p. 301; abbreviated English edition, *The First Book of the Bible: Genesis,* trans. by Ernest I. and Walter Jacob (New York: KTAV, 1974), p. 79.

6. The editing of the Flood Story is more complicated. A large block of material (6:1-9:27), consisting of a basically priestly story supplemented with old Epic material and a prologue (the angel marriages) and an epilogue (Noah's drunkenness), has been inserted into the heart of the Noachic genealogy (5:32 + 9:28-29) found in the toledoth document (ch. 5).

7. Gerhard von Rad, *Genesis,* Old Testament Library, trans. by John H. Marks (2nd ed., Philadelphia: Westminster Press, 1972), p. 152.

8. John Calvin, *Commentaries on the Book of Genesis,* I, trans. by John King (Grand Rapids, Mich.: Eerdmans, 1948), p. 332.

Roland Murphy

"Nation" in the Old Testament

ISRAEL, NATION AND PEOPLE

"NATION" and "people" are correlative rather than truly synonymous terms in Old Testament usage. Only in a few instances are the terms *gôy* (nation) and *'am* (people) interchangeable. The frequency of usage is also important: about 1800 instances of *'am* and 550 of *gôy*. What nuance can be attached to these terms? A study of the late E. Speiser still remains valid.[1] He pointed out that *gôy*, or nation, designates a group in terms of its political and territorial affiliation, whereas *'am*, or people, characterizes a group in terms of consanguinity. On this basis Israel was *both* a nation and a people. Thus the patriarchal promise (I will make of you a great *nation*; cf. Gen. 12:2; 18:17; 46:3) makes good sense. Abraham and the patriarchs belong to an extended family; the departure from Ur of the Chaldees was precisely for the purpose of establishing a nation. On the other hand, Israel was a *people*, God's people. In the Hebrew Bible *gôy* is never construed with the sacred name, Yahweh; in virtue of the election and covenant, Israel is the people (*'am*) of the Lord, not his *gôy*. In this sense, as Speiser remarks, the reference to Yahweh as a "national" God is not strictly correct. He is not bound to a locality as Enlil is with Nippur; he is bound to Israel as his people.

Indeed, Israel's importance is clearly religious, rather than political. Her existence as a political unit was short-lived. The federation of tribes (which from the beginning was never an ethnic unity), became a monarchy under Saul, David and Solomon, a period of about 100 years. The divided monarchy lasted 200 years for the northern kingdom of Israel (Samaria fell in 721), and a little over 300 years for the southern kingdom of Judah (Jerusalem fell in

71

587). But underlying this hazardous political existence was the covenant with the Lord, the unity of the people of God. It is not surprising that a shepherd from Tekoah in the south preaches in the north (Amos), or that a prophet of the northern kingdom was preserved and transmitted in the south (Hosea). The book of Deuteronomy certainly originated in the north, but it became the heart of the reform instituted by Josiah in the kingdom of Judah.[2] The sense of being the Lord's "special possession" (s^egullāh Exod. 19:5) is foremost in the Israelite consciousness. This identity has also been a prominent feature of theological study among Christians, for it undergirds the description of the Church as the new Israel and as the people of God.

From what we have said thus far, it appears that ethnic identity, the topic treated in the present issue of *Concilium*, is a reality which was never faced by Israel in the manner in which it presents itself to modern man. Even when Israel received political expression in terms of the divided monarchy, it remained a theocracy, with Yahweh as the true king. But are there any leads which the Old Testament provides for a theological assessment of ethnicity? I will indicate some important factors, which, however, must be interpreted against the background of Israel's identity as the people of God. This fact colors the sociological attitudes to neighbor that are expressed in the Old Testament in such a way as to make Israel's position unique. The mere translation of sociological attitudes from Israelite theocracy to twentieth-century democracy would be simplistic.

It must be admitted that the sense of being chosen, and the grant of the land of Canaan, contributed to a certain exclusivism in the heart of Israel. But it is the prophet Amos who served to keep Israel a bit off balance on this point. He wiped out any complacency by pointing out that election brought obligation, even punishment (Amos, 3:2), and he asked in a caustic rhetorical question,

> Are you not like the Ethiopians to me,
>   O men of Israel, says the Lord?
> Did I not bring the Israelites from the land of
>   Egypt
>   as I brought the Philistines from Caphtor
> and the Arameans from Kir? (Am. 9:7)

In the eyes of the Lord Israel has no more merit than the rest of the nations; he could have covenanted with any one of them (Deut. 7:8, "it was because the Lord loved you . . ."). Let not Israel forget that the Lord works across the whole canvas of history and peoples, including Israel's very enemies (Philistines, Arameans)!

ISRAEL AND THE NATIONS

Israel's historical role is played against the backdrop of the rich cultural legacy of the nations and peoples of the Fertile Crescent. In the Mesopotamian valley there are the successive waves of dominant peoples: Sumerians, Babylonians, Accadians, Neo-Babylonians, Persians, and eventually the Greeks and Romans. To the northwest lay the Hittite empire ("your father was an Amorite, and your mother a Hittite," Ezek. 16:3), and at the western end of the Crescent lay perennial Egypt. When Israel went in to possess the land of Canaan there was the reminder that this little corner of the earth was made up of "the Canaanites, the Hittites, the Hivites, the Perizzites, and the Girgashites, the Amorites, and the Jebusites" (Jos. 4:10). During its political existence Israel endured the threats of the Philistines, Arameans, Moabites and Edomites, not to mention the world empires. It is surely remarkable that Israel in the Table of Nations of Gen. 10 (discussed elsewhere in this issue of *Consilium*) attempted to identify itself in this maelstrom of peoples and cultures.

The dark side of Israel's attitude to the nations becomes evident in the phenomenon of doom war (Hebrew, *herem*), which is mentioned at several points in the narrative of the Conquest (e.g., Jos. 6-8, the Achan episode). The doom war, in which a whole population was wiped out as an act of homage to the deity, was conceived as an act of religion, a "holy war." This mentality Israel shared with its neighbors, as can be illustrated from the famous Moabite stone, where the same practice is mentioned. Theologians of another generation attempted to justify this as stemming from the direct will of God, to whom is to be attributed power over all life since he is the author of life. Such an explanation cannot satisfy anyone who is really trying to understand the Lord of the Old Testament. Rather, one must recognize here Israel's view of the will of the Lord, a view that was influenced by the cultural baggage of the ancient Near East. The divine tolerance of Israel's shortcomings in many other areas of moral conduct is apparent. There is no effort in the Old Testament to transform moral values overnight. Neither can modern humankind congratulate itself as having moved beyond the Old Testament view—not in this atomic world.

A similarly hostile attitude to the nations is manifested in the "oracles against the nations" which form part of several prophetical books (Is. 13-21, Jer. 46-51; Ezek. 25-32). The first two chapters of Amos are the most interesting example of the genre. The prophet makes a sweep around Damascus, Gaza, Tyre, Edom, Ammon, and Moab, condemning these peoples for their ferocious violence, and then he fittingly turns to Judah and Israel to indict them for their failure to observe the covenant stipulations. This phenomenon of oracles against the nations has its counterpart in the Egyptian execration texts—hostile wishes that were inscribed upon bowls, and directed against particular nations.

For the sake of completeness, one must also notice the unhappy incidents in the reform of Ezra and Nehemiah: the breakup of mixed marriages contracted between the Jews who had returned from exile and the women of neighboring territories (Ezra 9-10; Neh. 13.) The reform measures of these two men are at least understandable at this critical period of the birth of Judaism, and in view of Israel's past history. They need not be taken as normative for the entire Old Testament.

But there is another side to the story. Israel is not to be alone in sharing the divine blessing. It will become the true center for all nations:

> The mountain of the Lord's house
> > shall be established on the highest mountain
> > and raised above the hills.
> All nations shall stream toward it;
> > many peoples shall come and say:
> "Come, let us climb the Lord's mountain,
> > to the house of the God of Jacob,
> That he may instruct us in his ways,
> > and we may walk in his paths."
> For from Zion shall go forth instruction,
> > and the word of the Lord from Jerusalem" (Is. 2:2-3).

It is to the nations that the Servant of the Lord is commissioned:

> Here is my servant whom I uphold,
> > my chosen one with whom I am pleased,
> Upon whom I have put my spirit;
> > he shall bring forth justice to the nations . . .
> A bruised reed he shall not break,
> > and a smoldering wick he shall not quench,
> Until he establishes justice on the earth;
> > the coastlands will wait for his teaching (Is. 42:1-4).

Ultimately there is to be one king and one people; the nations dispersed after the tower of Babel will come together in a new unity, and "the earth shall be filled with the knowledge of the Lord, as waters cover the sea" (Is. 11:9).

ETHNIC IDENTIY AND ANCIENT ISRAEL

The modern issue of ethnicity can be illustrated from the Old Testament if one penetrates the unity which the covenant created for the people of God, i.e., by analyzing tribal identity within the people and by examining Israel's attitude toward strangers in its midst. Tribal identity never disappeared, and early on it contributed powerfully to the dissolution of the monarchy after Solomon. In the days of Jephthah the ascendancy of the tribe of Ephraim made itself felt (Jgs. 8:1 ff.). David's rise to the throne was secured by the approach of his kingship (2 Sam. 5:1 ff.). The division between northern and southern tribes was never eliminated by Solomon, despite a reorganization of the country that cut across tribal lines (1 Kgs. 12:16). The biblical evidence underlines the enduring strength of tribal identity down to the Restoration. Only then do the people present a more unified front. Judah is the heart of the restored group (Ezra 1:5), and an ever-increasing religious identity emerges (Neh. 13). It is interesting to note the change in the meaning of "the people of the land" ('am hā' āres) at this time. Whereas it previously designated the whole body of citizens that enjoyed civic rights in a given area, it came to mean the non-Jewish residents of Palestine who opposed the restoration of Judah. Thus the phrase was oriented to the meaning it would acquire in the rabbinic period: those who are ignorant of the Law.

The presence of several foreigners within Israel deserves notice. The man wronged by David's adultery is Uriah the Hittite. It is surely significant that David's wrongdoing is not palliated by Uriah's foreign extraction (cf. Nathan's parable in 2 Sam. 12). David's own bodyguard was made up of foreigners (the Cherethites and Pelethites), a veritable foreign legion, and "600 men of Gath" who accompanied him from the city when the king was forced to flee at the revolt of Absalom (2 Sam. 15:18 ff.). The name of one of his loyal servants has been preserved for us in the stirring episode of David's retreat from Jerusalem: Ittai the Gittite. When David offers him the opportunity to stay and throw in his lot with Absalom, he gives as reasons that he is both foreigner and exile from his own country (e.i., Gath). But Ittai nobly swears by the Lord and casts his lot with David, "whether for death or for life."

A foreigner who lived more or less permanently within Israel was called a gēr, or resident alien. These were originally non-Israelite inhabitants of the land who were not assimilated by marriage, and who were recognized as having certain rights without being full citizens. Many of the laws reflect concern for this group which labored under the disadvantage of not sharing in the distribution of the land. They were not to be oppressed because Israel was itself once a resident alien in Egypt (Exod. 22:21; 23:9). Indeed, the Israelites were to love the gērîm as themselves (Lev. 19:34). In his vision of the restored people Ezekiel (47:22-23) sees them as totally assimilated to the Israelites, enjoying the same rights. The institution of the resident aliens prepared the way, as de Vaux points out,[3] for the proselytes, or God-fearers, of the post-exilic period, i.e., gentiles who were associated with Judaism as sort of catechumens.

The hostility of Israel against the surrounding nations has been described above, but this must be counterbalanced by certain examples which prove that foreign ethnic identity was not incompatible with being a member of the people of God. "Ruth, the Moabite," is almost a catch-phrase in ch. 2 of the book of Ruth, where it introduces and ends (vv. 1,22) the scene at the barley harvest, and it is repeated significantly in the legal transaction at the city gate where Boaz takes Ruth as wife (4:5-10). Ruth's national identity remains uppermost in the reader's consciousness. It is all the more significant that this identity blends easily with her new home and religion, as is suggested by her words to Naomi (1:16): "wherever you go, I will go, wherever you lodge, I will lodge, your people will be my people, and your God my God."

The book of Jonah also speaks to this topic. First of all, the theological lesson is that the Lord's love and concern for humankind is not tied down by the covenant with Israel. It flows out and beyond the covenanted people to embrace even their hated enemies, such as the Assyrians, whose forces destroyed Samaria in 721. The Assyrians remain Assyrians, but they are portrayed as doing penance, from king to commoner and the Lord "relents" (3:9-10—a motif taken over from Jer. 18:8-10). The Assyrians of chs. 3-4 are the pendant to the unidentified but pagan sailors of ch. 1 who pray first each to his own God (v. 5), but who eventually offer sacrifices and vows to Yahweh (1:16).

CONCLUSION

From what has been said, it is clear that the biblical view of nation in the Old Testament has several inherent ambiguities. Israel's hostility to the nations can be accounted for in terms of several factors: oppression by surrounding nations and world empires, the seduction which foreign religions had for Israel, the growing exclusivism which characterized early Judaism. But against this we have noted many points of openness towards the nations (the books of Ruth, Jonah, etc.). One must avoid the danger of selectivity and acknowledge the complexity of the data provided by the Old Testament.

On the other hand, one should stress the recognition of the rights of foreign groups within the people of God (the "resident alien," the attitudes manifested in the books of Ruth and Jonah). These are perhaps singular, but they are also telling, and directive. The strains of universalism, of pluralism within unity, are present. The task remains for the people of God: to meditate upon these insights and thereby to move on to further horizons. In ways peculiar to itself Israel achieved a global consciousness which is a challenge to us all.

Notes

1. " 'People' and 'Nation' of Israel," *Journal of Biblical Literature* 79 (1960),

(1960), pp. 157-163.

2. Cf. R.E. Murphy, "Deuteronomy—A Document of Revival," *Concilium* 89, pp. 26—36.

3. *Ancient Israel* (New York: NcGraw-Hill, 1965) 1:70-72.

Bruce Vawter

Universalism in
the New Testament

AS a correspondent wrote in the *Times Literary Supplement* some years ago, "Nationalism was, and is, a disease of the nineteenth and twentieth centuries." To take nationalism as a disease is, certainly, to take it at its worst: it was the purpose of the author to trace "a certain logical progression" from nationalistic scholarship and science which could deem all other scholarship and science peripheral to the virulence of master-race praxis under which all other peoples became peripheral. In this sense of the word it can be fairly said that nationalism was practically unknown in the world into which the New Testament was born and that in this respect, therefore, the supranationalism of the New Testament is rather the product of its age than a challenge to it.

To be sure, the world of the New Testament was the world of Roman arrogance and of Jewish rebellion, in both of which nationalism obviously played a part. More typically, however, it was the world which the Roman genius for order—and road-building—had organized about the dream of Alexander—perhaps the most successfully realized dream in history of any world ruler with perhaps the best reason to be remembered as "the Great"—and had created that curious syncretism that we know as Hellenism. Curious, because those who were supposedly conquered, philosophically and politically, became in some sense the conquerors: the Olympian gods disappeared in favor of the Egyptian and Oriental deities who had been made their counterparts, and Rome, as Tacitus held, became the place "where all things hideous and shameful from every part of the world find their center and become popular." Historians in Egypt and Babylonia—we know two of them as Manetho and Berossos—were inspired by the spirit of Greek enquiry to research the dimly recalled traditions of their own peoples which had long languished uncherished, and then throw them into the common melting pot. They wrote in Greek, of course, not only because it was the *lingua franca* of their world but also because only in this language had thoughts occurred and words been formed that evoked the retrieval of these traditions. Greece was the heaven of Hellenism and its administrator, but the phenomenon of Hellenism itself was the emergence of a new and other world that was the closest thing to a cosmopolis that we are ever likely to see in this universe.

The Jewish nation (*ethnos*, to use the contemporary expression) made no exception to the general syncretic rule. Both the Jews of the Diaspora or of Palestine who wrote in Greek and who consciously tried to accommodate Judaism to Hellenism—Philo, Josephus, the author of 2 Maccabees, the author of the Wisdom of Solomon—as well as those Jews who wrote in Hebrew and on purely religious grounds opposed some aspects of Hellenism—the author of 1 Maccabees, Ben Sira, the fathers of the Talmud—had embraced one and all most of the essentials of the world-view Alexander sought to propagate. Even the most separatist of the Jewish traditions had, consciously or not, succumbed to or even anticipated in their own fashion Hellenism's internationalism of ideas. The Priestly stratum in the Old Testament, the very one which is most adamant about the laws of ritual purity and external observance that distinguished Jew from Gentile, is likewise the one which tried to erase ancestral hatreds of Edomite and Arab and to make room for that catholic Judaism which Isaiah 55:1–56:8 proclaimed. The sectaries of Qumran, as exclusivist interpreters of Judaism as it is possible to imagine, nevertheless reveal themselves to have drunk more deeply and perhaps more indiscriminately than many others from the ferment of exotic ideas stirred up first by the Persian and then the Hellenistic dominations of Palestine. It has also been plausibly argued that the Pharisees, those "normative" Jews who built a fence about the Law and did most to resist foreign intrusion, in the long run because of their acceptance of the principles of development, adaptation, and reinterpretation, were the children of Hellenism far more than the fundamentalist Sadducees, though it was the latter who freely assimilated to the ways and customs of the Gentiles.

In other words, when Christianity first appeared as a Jewish sect, it did not need, or it did not very much need, to become persuaded of the universal potential of its gospel. There was nothing parallel to the situation of Muhammad, whose dream of a universal brotherhood based on faith, the *umma muslima*, was conceived precisely against the backdrop of Arab blood ties and tribal loyalties for which he wished to substitute, and who was genuinely surprised when Jews and Christians did not join in his effort. The New Testament is historically honest when it portrays Jesus as having had a mission confined to the Jews of Galilee and Judea; but neither has it romanticized the facts when it maintains that this mission was rightly and inevitably turned into a mission to all mankind not by any imposition of extraneous ideologies—the nineteenth-century myth of the Hellenizing Paul, for example—but simply out of a dynamism that it had already inherited from Judaism.

Of course, there was and is a universalism professed by Christianity that is not professed by Judaism and never was, not even in its times of proselytism; and of course this universalism is owed to something other than the Judaism of Christianity's origins. It cannot be accounted for, however, by recourse to the modern scholastic dogma of development from Palestinian Judaism through Hellenistic Judaism into Gentile Hellenism, through which process Christianity, its ideas, and its vocabulary are supposed to have been successively transformed and reinterpreted. The classic statement of New Testament universalism that sunders it both from the Jewish and Gentile worlds of its time is that of Gal. 3:28: "There does not exist among you Jew or Greek, slave or freeman, male or female. All are one in Christ Jesus." This is the assertion of one who in Phil. 3:5 characterized himself as circumcised on the eighth day, Israelite by race, of the tribe of Benjamin, a Hebrew of Hebrews, and according to the Law a Pharisee. It is the assertion of an early, not of a late New Testament Christian, and of one whose connections with Judaism are very proximate. Yet we may wonder whether early or late within the time-frame of New Testament composition has any really significant meaning. A half-century after Paul what we now know as the First Gospel would be portraying Jesus for a Christian audience as a teacher of Torah, one of the great Aboth, as though the connection with Judaism had never been broken at all. So it is with the Epistle of James. But with the Johannine literature, also very "late," we are confronted with a rupture with Judaism so pronounced that even in an evidently Jewish writing "the Jews" has become an alien and pejorative term. This mixture of contradictories indicates several things. On the one hand, as Walter Bauer pointed out long ago, Christianity was not in its inception one theology only but several. But on the other hand, as Bauer did not adequately perceive there was a unity in the various theologies of primitive Christianity that marked it a new outpouring of the Spirit of God. Matthew's Gospel, after all, for all its portrayal along with Qumran of Jesus as Teacher of Righteousness, likewise puts the age of Israel in the past and superseded and ends with the Great Commission which is one of the most universalistic pronouncements in the New Testament.

The universalism of the New Testament which was really new as far as Judaism was concerned was its abolition of the distinction between Jew and Gentile, or "Greek," as the language of the time drew the distinction. This distinction was not nationalistic but religious and cultural. It was a distinction that even the most ecumenical type of Judaism had never been able to eradicate, even with its best intentions. In part, of course, it was founded on language, as the Hebrew-Hellenist dichotomy of Acts 6:1 makes plain. Here the Jewish Christians "who spoke Greek" are opposed to "those who spoke the language of the Jews." That there should have been controversy between such culturally divided people is entirely understandable then as it is now in a culturally divided America, in the barrios and ghettos of Chicago or New York; and it is also a historical datum for the Jerusalem of the first Christian century, since we know that at least one Greek-speaking synagogue existed there. But the major distinction was not Hebrew and Hellenist, Jews distinguished by the language they spoke, but rather Jew or Greek, that is, Jews born to the name and those who were not, who perforce were Greek because the world was Greek and who could never become Jews because they had not been born Jews, even if they had become Jews in religion through proselytism or the semiproselytism of those Gentiles "who feared God," that is, who accepted the moral code of Judaism and its elevated concept of Deity without bringing themselves to submit to ritual circumcision and the other particularities of Jewish practice that constituted the Jews a peculiar people in their world. Jewish rites were frequently caricatured by the Romans, as they would be later in Christian times. However, there was also that about them, even when fairly understood, which conflicted with the accepted mores: the Jews observed festal days, but always at the wrong times, and they held in abhorrence the prime animal of sacrifice, the pig. They were certainly not equipped to become a world religion as long as they held to cultural taboos and particularist traditions which could strike no chord in the experience of the rest of mankind with which they expected to relate and to empathize. Christianity quickly did what Judaism was unwilling to do, and in doing so it speeded the division of the two into separate religions. Christianity abolished the dietary laws and declared nul and void any distinction of access to the gospel based on prior cultural or ethnic descent—that distinction that is so paramount in the New Testament texts (cf. Acts 14:1; 16:1, 3; 17:4; 18:4; 19:10, 7; 20:21; 21:28; Rom. 1:14-16; 2:9-10; 10:12; 1 Cor. 1:22-24; 10:32; 12:13). How this was finally done we do not know exactly, since the New Testament is not at one on the subject; probably it was done differently in the various churches where the need arose. That it was indeed done marked the beginning of a new universalism and the demise of an older attempt at universalism from which it had been born, which latter now turned more and more in on itself and produced an entirely different kind of religious witness to the world.

The transcendence of the social distinction between slave and free which Paul confidently ascribed to the common Christian calling is perhaps that ideal which is most susceptible of interpretation as theoretical rather than practical in the early Christian conscience. Or, if not merely theoretical, certainly not part of any program for social change or for radical departure from the existing order of things. One would be hard pressed to offer any proof that the New Testament did anything whatever to alter the presumption of its time that slavery was the established and ordained lot of a great proportion of mankind, just as it is patently impossible to show that it ever seriously affected the thinking of the later Christian peoples who built up their economies in Europe, Africa, the Americas, and elsewhere, premised on the institution of slavery. Christian apologists in later times have been fond of the notion that it was a New Testament ideal that did eventually, painfully, and gradually permeate society and lead to the abolition of slavery. If there is something to be said for this contention, it can only be admitted that the process was indeed painful and gradual, since it was just about a century ago that acknowledged slavery disappeared in Christian lands. (About unacknowledged slavery we need not speak.) And not too much cynicism is required to point out that when acknowledged slavery did at last go, it went by imposition of fiat from without, a fiat which was admittedly inspired partially by a secularized notion of the rights of man owing something to the tradition of Judaeo-Christianity but inspired much more by the practical fact of life that the anti-slavery powers which stamped the institution out would otherwise have been at the economic mercy of those who depended on slavery for their survival.

In the Epistle to Philemon Paul returns the fugitive slave Onesimus to his master, pleading that he be received "no longer as a slave but as more than a slave, a beloved brother, especially dear to me; and how much more than a brother to you, since now you will know him both as a man and in the Lord" (vs. 16). This expresses a lofty ideal of the commonalty of mankind, but it would obviously go beyond the evidence to suggest, as some commentators have, that Paul was urging Philemon to the manumission of Onesimus. Paul's invocation of common humanity and of religious dimension within which that humanity should be evaluated hardly exceeds the thought that had long ago occurred to the author of Job 31:13-15. The school of Epicurus, destined to be ridiculed uncritically by both Jewish and Christian observers, included both slaves and women among its pupils on an equal footing with freemen who sought to find in it a philosophy and way of life.

We are forced to add that neither in the Liberation Theology of South America and of the Third World do we discern any late flowering of a freedom-bearing seed planted by the New Testament. Liberation theology has uttered eloquent words with respect to the mechanics of oppression and exploitation and has become a powerful witness to the haves in favor of the have-nots, telling the former truths which they would not otherwise tell themselves. It has done this, however, largely in terms of Marxist dialectic. There is nothing necessarily wrong with Marxist dialectic, but it is not the New Testament. What we miss in liberation theology is the biblical—chiefly Old Testament—concern for the individual human being and his personal responsibility as opposed to his pertinence to a class, exploiting or exploited, and we also miss a concern for the right of dissent against the power of the state or majority, however enlightened or right thinking that majority may be. Neither in the earlier nor in the later Christian attitudes towards human bondage or freedom, therefore, does the New Testament seem to have played much of a role.

As far as New Testament times themselves are concerned, it is probably fairly stated that a liberating word was not the necessity that it later became. Neither in Judaism nor in the Hellenistic world was slavery the utterly barbarous, dehumanizing instrument that it became in the ages we call Christian. Both in Judaism and in Hellenism, whatever the legalities, the slave was a person, a human being, frequently enough the respected tutor of his masters. He was in an unfortunate position politically and economically, though he also frequently had means to redress the balance. He was not, as his later counterparts of the Indies or Africa became through the greed of fellow tribesmen, Arab entrepreneurs, and European traffickers, a simple chattel to whom no human qualities were allowed. This is the kind of slavery that existed in the United States of America at the very time that it declared as self-evident that all men are created equal, endowed by their Creator with certain unalienable rights, among which are life, liberty, and the pursuit of happiness. The American founding fathers were not conscious hypocrites; it simply never occurred to many of them to consider their black slaves the beneficiaries of the rights of man. In just the opposite way, it would not have occurred to Paul ever to consider that slaves were different from any other men in the matter of right and dignity.

Something of a similar qualification must be made of the New Testament's equation of men and women under the gospel. Gal. 3:28 evidently envisaged an equality that would fall far short of what now is considered a minimum. 1 Tim. 2:11-15 can take a very patronizing tone in dealing with the conduct of women in the church (not to mention 1 Tim. 3:11, which strongly hints that of woman is to be expected those vices which male bias has simply ascribed to her gratuitously: a self-fulfilling prophecy); but even 1 Cor. 14:33b-36, which is Paul and not an imitator of Paul, clearly regards woman as an inferior creature, one to be cajoled, respected, cosseted, all these, yet not taken seriously in a one-for-one dialogue along with her consort. Does it suffice to observe that while Judaism did not allow the teaching of Torah to women, Christianity did, even in this mitigated way? Possibly so; but if so, it was a small advance.

The fact is, that while in strict law Judaism allowed practically no rights to women, in fact they more than the solemn rabbis determined and controlled Jewish tradition, as they still do. It is very questionable that any right was conceded in Christianity to any Jewish woman that she did not already possess and enjoy under the Torah. The Wisdom literature and some of the history of the Old Testament, a better index to what really was than are its laws, which merely stated what ought to be, leave us in no doubt about this. As for Gentile society, it is doubtless safe to say that less rather than more freedom was the lot of the woman who entered the Christian community.

In sum, the universalism professed by the New Testament contained nothing shocking, revolutionary, or fraught with social consequence. It took the directions indicated by the best in the traditions on which it could draw, necessarily breaking with the one here or there in favor of the other. Its success lay more in assimilation than in innovation, in confirmation rather than negation of empirical human ideals. In doing so, of course, it allowed a climate for the further fructifying of these ideals. The best efforts of Christianity subsequent to the New Testament that have been rewarded with comparable success have attempted neither more nor less than this.

John Shea

Reflections on Ethnic Consciousness and Religious Language

INTRODUCTION

OBVIOUS truths, when they hit, have the greatest impact. One such truth which is currently crashing into consciousness is that no one is neutral. Data is not impartially gathered and collated. Hidden principles of selection are always at work, including and excluding according to their preferences. All observation is theory-laden; all experience is appropriated through structures of awareness which employ elaborate filters. The naked encounter of the self with reality is a romantic fiction. The attempt to move behind all language and symbol, the lens of perception, is futile. This insight does not destroy objectivity. It merely redefines it.

In this atmosphere it is only fitting to "put the cards on the table." Before the discussion begins it is helpful to try to name the controlling images and constructs which guide a person's thought, to surface the assumptive world present and operative in all his observations. In other words, to situate is not something that is done "at last" after the ideas and feelings have been heard but "at first" to provide a deeper understanding of the issues. The attempt to situate is an ambiguous project. Placement can be a way of dismissal. To situate a theological effort can become a way of pre-empting it from serious consideration. Once a theological effort is located, critical points become predictable. From past performances it is known what will be defended, or better yet, what will not be yielded. The reductionist slogans are at hand: Roman Catholic authoritarianism, neo-orthodox isolationism, the lingering positivism of linguistic analysis, etc. But placement can also be an effort of respect. Its purpose is not to foreclose on a theological effort but to understand more deeply the values and perspectives which guide it. It is an attempt to appropriate the internal frame of reference of a theologian and allow his thought its logic and power within that frame before challenging alternative frames are presented. In contemporary developmental models of dialogue this initial step is absolutely necessary if interchange is to be creative.

This situating effort, not seen as prejudice but as possibility, complements a central insight of ethnic consciousness. For ethnic consciousness where you came from makes a difference, in some cases all the difference. And so by way of an introduction to reflections on ethnic consciousness and religious language it is helpful to briefly state the ethnic and religious background of the person who writes these words.

I am a 34-year-old, third generation, Irish-American Catholic. I grew up on the west side of Chicago in a tight knit Catholic neighborhood. The Catholic school system I "went through" while in some respects inhibiting was basically an atmosphere of security, conscience, and freedom. I do not go along with the current fashion of scapegoating immigrant Catholicism for being repressive. It was a good environment to grow up in. I always knew I was Irish but I never reflectively interpreted myself as Irish. When I began to, my ethnicity did not come to me as a shock from the outside but as a surprise from within. It was like finding a diamond in your pocket.

ETHNIC CONSCIOUSNESS

In the United States the rise of ethnic consciousness is, in many cases, a response to the problem of identity. The previous most popular response to this problem, which over the long haul proved ineffective, was career. Since a major cause of the problem of identity was the highly transient society which business and industry promoted, it was understandable, if not exactly logical, that the solution would be sought in the careerism which these enterprises encouraged. In this situation the question of identity subtly shifts from who are you to what do you do. Among the male population career began to equal self-worth and any crisis in the career had immediate and deep resonances in the psyche. But even the most promising careers devolve into ordinary jobs. Work, however rewarding, is not capable of answering the probing questions of identity which the human person asks. It is not that people do not passionately pursue medicine, law, engineering, etc. They do and always will. It is that the career has not delivered what it promised—integration, peace, self-worth. It does not tell me who I am but merely what I do and, in most cases, what I have to do for food, clothing, and shelter. Career is not the balm for the identity ache.

The turning away from a career solution toward an ethnic handling of identity was strikingly symbolized for me at a recent wake. Joe Moriarity was well past the time when he should have died, so he did. At the wake the younger Irish males passed the coffin, prayed, and went next door to the tavern to figure things out. They were all successful in their various careers—Irish on the way up. They were basically martini drinkers but in honor of Joe everyone had a shot and a beer. There was not much lament for Joe but there was for what was going out of the world with him. Joe, it was said over and over again in a thousand different ways, knew who he was. He had a sense of solidarity, roots, a basis for firm judgment. His world was demarcated without being closed; his values were sure without being arrogant. Joe, who in his entire lifetime did not make as much money as these men do in five years, was envied. These men took their careers for granted and began to probe their Irish-Catholic background for a sense of who they were. Scenes like this, perhaps not as explicit, are happening more and more.

There are two aspects of this emerging ethnic consciousness which have a special potential for religious language. The first is particularity. Ethnic consciousness is more than another facet of the "return to experience" movement. Ethnic consciousness wants to appropriate experience in its most concrete configuration. It is not satisfied to talk about "love." It wants to show the tonalities and passion of love in an Italian-American or Irish-American or Polish-American or Black-American setting. For ethnic consciousness to say love concerns the well-being of the neighbor is a hopeless abstraction. Love is a mother who is trying to possess and trying to let go and is torn in the trying. Love is the things husbands and wives do to each other in their passionate attempts to care. For Irish-American ethnic consciousness a treatise on love is not *De Caritate* but Eugene O'Neill's *Moon for the Misbegotten*. Love is filled with the trickery of an old father to find a man for his spinster daughter, the bravado of the aging daughter, the dreams of a suitor who cannot rid himself of guilt or find the strength to respond to the love that is offered. In the first moment ethnic consciousness wants to appropriate experience in its sights and smells and sounds. Because of this, the favored medium of communications for ethnic consciousness is the story.

Particularity is the guardian of mystery. If the concrete shape of the experience is clung to, the mind cannot smooth out the wrinkles too quickly. Particularity does not easily admit of answers but continues to test ways of dealing with the questions. When concrete experience is maintained, the mysterious always has a reference point. The human story is the natural locale of unbidden gifts, strange reversals, hidden centers of concern, a sense of responding to life. Logic does not yet rule in this consciousness so the person is open to the "more-than-logic" which is present. Ethnic consciousness is a battle against abstraction and to the extent that it is successful it merges with the concerns of religious language.

A second aspect of ethnic consciousness which indicates a way of reclaiming religious language is community. The locus of ethnic consciousness is family and race. The focus is not on the individual in his quest for truth and meaning but on the relationships that sustain him or break him. The perspective on the person is not solitary and his problems and possibilities are not his sole possession. He is the center and product of an intimate bonding process (family, relatives and friends), and a racial inheritance (the characteristics and traits of grandparents and great-grandparents). This aspect of ethnic consciousness emphasizes the inescapable relatedness of the human person. As particularity is a reaction against abstraction, community is a reaction against an isolated individualism.

Before considering how these two emphases of ethnic consciousness provide an entry into religious language, two paradoxes of ethnic consciousness should be briefly mentioned. On the surface ethnic consciousness can appear as a form of racism. The emphasis on particularity can be seen as isolating group from group, fostering the differences within the human community, and leading to oppression and hostility. There is no doubt that a partial approach to ethnic consciousness could lead to chauvinism. But a "thoroughgoing" ethnicity, respecting every heritage and in its unique appropriation of what it means to be human, could lead to a respect which is the beginning of dialogue. Too quickly saying we are alike can lead to the violent discovery that we are not. But if each story is told in its ethnic particularity, we may see patterns of similarity, complementary rhythms of sin and redemption, and be bound together as storytellers. The second paradox concerns the quest for identity. To an extent ethnic consciousness reverses the aggressive, panicky style that often characterizes this search. The question is not who am I but who are we? The anxiety the identity question raises is mollified because it is shared. The answer is not a conquest but a gift, received in interaction with others, and not in solitary introspection. The problem of racism and identity receive a subtle, but promising, reversal when appropriated through ethnic consciousness.

RELIGIOUS LANGUAGE

Many problems concerning religious language can be clarified by distinguishing between the established religious vocabulary and a religious use of ordinary language. On the level of the local church in the United States the cultural mood of "hard empiricism" has twisted religious language into observational words. The enshrined religious vocabulary—God, Christ, Sin, Grace, Kingdom—designate objects outside the person which can be discovered and tagged. This mood induces a flat-minded literalism. Religious language is not allowed to function symbolically but is frozen into statement of facts. Religious symbols do not configure and mobilize human experience but are considered solely as independent entities susceptible to detached scrutiny. This form of "supernatural positivism" has rendered the traditional symbols ineffective. The task is to revitalize the established vocabulary through an understanding of how language is used religiously.

A religious use of language does not concentrate on a special vocabulary. Its contention is that religious language is not a separate language but the way language is used. Two central characteristics of a religious use of language can be outlined. The first, and most important, is its multivalent nature. Religious language refers to finite interactions and to a sacred and transcendent dimension which is manifest through the finite references. A classic example is the tree in Druid religion. The tree is a finite reality but through it the sacred manifests itself. A second characteristic is that religious language is concerned with the ultimate meaning of our comings and goings. It highlights our basic affirmation or negation of life, our freedom and solidarity, and our responsibility and salvation. When language exhibits these two traits, it is being used religiously.

The twin focus of ethnic consciousness on particularity and community encourages a religious use of language. When human consciousness is not plunged into the particular and the relational but comfortable in abstraction and isolation, it is tempted to flatten multi-dimensional experience. It is sensitive to one-to-one relationships but has no feel for the Mystery, the More, the Whole, the Encompassing which is the felt context of the particular and the relational. In much of contemporary discussion transcendence is a self-generating activity, initiated from within and not in response to Being. With this understanding there is no need to use language religiously because life is not experienced religiously. Ethnic consciousness, on the other hand, because it lays hold of experience in its most particular configuration is attuned to the larger Mystery which permeates and contextualizes all finite interactions. Ethnic emphasis on the concrete encourages three-point aware-ness—knower, known, and the Mystery in which both participate. A religious use of language attempts to capture this sensitivity.

The ethnic focus on the relational is especially suited to reveal the transcendent dimension of human experience. In *Man Becoming* Gregory Baum unpacks the transcendent awareness that is present in the activities of dialogue and community. Man comes to be in dialogue with others. Out of this ongoing dialogue a man develops a sense of who he is and where he is going. Men speak to each other words of acceptance and love but they also speak painful words that call for conversion and new life styles. In and through these human words a special word is spoken, a word which transcends the people involved. This word is discerned as transcendent and gratuitous because the speaker knows that it is not necessarily his alone and that by it he himself is judged. The same awareness is present in communion. Man in communion with other people is loved and accepted. In this love and acceptance he finds the strength to reply to the special word of conversion offered him. This love and acceptance which is the core of man's freedom is a gift given him by others. But here again man senses that the gift of human communion goes beyond it, transcends human ambiguity and frailty. Man knows that the gift dimension of life is more than he is. Ethnic consciousness with its emphasis on the relational provides a perspective within which religious sensitivity is possible and a religious use of language meaningful.

Besides ethnic consciousness facilitating the multivalent character of religious language, it powerfully presents the ultimate questions of life. In abstract and individualized formulations our plans proceed smoothly, our ideals are enacted with little trouble, our kingdoms come without crosses. Ultimate questions remain in the background because proximate affairs are moving with uninterrupted logic. But when experience is appropriated in its particular and relational configuration, contradictions and obstinacies enter. We find a strange betrayal within us. The ideal plan we chose to follow we suddenly desert. At the center of our confessed love there is manipulation; in the midst of our dialogue there is domination; at the heart of our major truth a lie lurks. When we are immersed in the concrete relational world, we cannot escape the ultimate questions of sin and redemption, of guilt and forgiveness, of purpose and salvation.

The dual focus of ethnic consciousness on the particular and the relational lends itself to a religious appropriation of human experience and a consequent religious use of language. Through this consciousness, therefore, it becomes possible to designate the range of experience which renders the traditional Christian symbols meaningful. But influences travel in both directions. As ethnic consciousness provides an awareness that calls for religious language, the Christian religious symbols provide an interpretation which ethnic experience desperately needs. Through the Christian symbols ethnic experience is discerned in both its sinful and graced moments, in its false prides and true possibilities. In short, ethnic consciousness is a way of claiming the meaningfulness of Christian religious symbols and Christian religious symbols are a way of claiming the truthfulness of ethnic experience. The continued interaction of ethnic consciousness and Christian religious symbols is a promising endeavor.

David Tracy

Ethnic Pluralism and
Systematic Theology: Reflections

I. INTRODUCTION: DEFINITIONS

A theological discussion of ethnicity demands a clarification of at least three terms: ethnicity, society, and theology. Since neither the extensive literature on ethnicity nor that on theology yields common definitions, it seems imperative to clarify the definitions employed in this article. The realities of space-limitation, however, force a brief statement of the definitions chosen as assumptions of the discussion rather than the supporting arguments for each choice:

1. *Ethnicity* may be understood as religious, racial, national, linguistic, and geographic diversity in American society.[1] This definition confines the discussion to American society and eliminates "class" considerations. This definition also assumes that "race," although not confined to ethnic categories, does possess an ethnic dimension. The present discussion of ethnicity will thereby focus upon the distinct cultural value-orientations involved in diverse ethnic perspectives. "Class," "race," and "sex" (and thereby the social realities of "class-conflict," "racism," and "sexism") remain relevant considerations to an analysis of American society, but are bracketed from the present consideration. These factors could not be bracketed indefinitely, of course, from any exhaustive discussion of American society or of contemporary theology.

2. *Society* may be understood in relatively non-theory-laden terms as composed of three "realms":[2]

(a) The realm of the *techno-economic structure* is concerned with the organization and allocation of goods and services. This structure frames the occupation and stratification systems of the society and uses modern *technology* for instrumental ends.

(b) The realm of the *polity* is concerned with the legitimate meanings of social justice and the use of power. This involves the control of the *legitimate* use of force and the regulation of conflict (in libertarian societies within the rule of law), in order to achieve the particular conceptions of justice embodied in a society's traditions or its constitution.

(c) The realm of *culture* (chiefly art and religion, and reflection upon both in philosophy and theology) is concerned with symbolic expressions. Those expressions, whether originating or reflective, attempt to explore and express the meaning and values of human existence, both individual, group, and communal.

The question of ethnicity is principally relevant for a discussion of the realm of "culture"—and thereby involves, as we shall see below, a discussion of "cultural justice." A theological clarification of ethnic factors in the realm of "culture" should also bear import for a discussion of social polity issues. This article, however, will focus its attention upon the "cultural justice" issue and merely indicate the relevance to "justice in the polity" (ordinarily called social justice issues) implied by this discussion.

3. *Christian theology*, in its most general definition, is that discipline which involves reflection upon the meanings present in human experience and the meanings present in the Christian tradition.[3] All theological reflection is articulated in one of three analogous public forms.

(a) A first kind of "public" theology (ordinarily labelled fundamental theology) investigates and correlates—principally from a philosophical viewpoint—the meanings of our *common* human experience and the meanings of the Christian tradition. This form of theological discourse is principally related to that community of inquiry called the "academy" and to those modes of reasoned discourse and argument which bear the primary and obvious meaning of a "public" discussion open to all reasonable persons.

(b) A second kind of "public" theology (ordinarily called systematic theology) articulates the disclosive and transformative possibilities of a particular religious tradition to a wider public. The social base of systematic theologians, therefore, is ordinarily a particular church tradition (here understood as a community of moral and religious commitment and discourse).

(c) A third kind of "public" theology (ordinarily called "practical" theology) will articulate the disclosive and transformative possibilities of a particular cultural heritage or a particular social, cultural, or political movement to a wider, pluralistic society. Most forms of both "liberation" theologies and "ethnic" theologies seem to use this model of the theological task.

My own position is that any properly theological reflection upon any significant cultural phenomenon logically involves the theologian in all three tasks of theology and thereby in all three parent communities (academy, church, and cultural heritage or movement).

In sum, this interpretation of the task of theology and the reality of ethnicity demands that the present systematic reflections concentrate upon the "cultural" realm of ethnic values from the perspective of a "systematic" theology informed by both "fundamental" and "practical" concerns. More specifically, such theological reflection upon ethnic cultural values must face the following three strictly theological concerns: (1) the meaning of ethnic "experience" for theology; (2) the meaning of ethnic "pluralism" for theology; (3) the meaning and character of strictly Christian theological principles in relationship to any particular ethnic value-system.

II. THEOLOGY, ETHNICITY AND EXPERIENCE

Thesis: Ethnic experience is a legitimate source of theological reflection; any classical expression of a particular ethnic religious heritage possesses a public, not private character.

A hallmark of most forms of contemporary theology is their insistence upon experience as a source of theological reflection. When employed by philosophical (usually fundamental) theologians, the appeal to experience is most often to a religious dimension of our *common* human experience. The reality of the latter can be defended on general philosophical grounds, ordinarily involving both phenomenological and transcendental moments.

When this same appeal to experience is made by systematic and practical theologians the referent is ordinarily an explicit and specific set of religious experiences of a particular Christian tradition. From this point of view, ethnic experience can serve as a summary expression for an historically conscious retrieval of a particular cultural and religious heritage. In sum, the two constants of most forms of contemporary theology (viz. some appeal to "experience" and an explicit affirmation of modern historical consciousness) are both present in the more recent appeal to one's ethnic experience as a source for theology. For an appeal to ethnic experience is a heightening of consciousness of one's own relationship to a particular cultural apprehension of values, including religious values.

The most frequent rejoinder to the latter appeal is the familiar charge that Christianity's universalist meaning will be endangered by being reduced to a series of particularist religious options. Christian theology, in its turn, will be reduced to a disparate series of particularist cultural expressions, for each ethnic theology will bear little if any intrinsic relationship to the others. In sum, Christian theology, which should possess a public, indeed a universal, character, may retreat into a congeries of "private" ethnic theologies. The Tower of Babel will be rebuilt under theological auspices.

This familiar suspicion seriously misunderstands the phenomenon of "ethnic theologies" on two counts. First, as the third thesis will clarify, any theologically responsible ethnic theology does not really reduce "Christian" experience to its ethnic cultural embodiment. Indeed, such explicitly Christian culturally incarnated *and* transcendent principles as grace-sin; faith as gift or event; faith-reason; love and justice remain present in all responsible ethnic theologies. These principles challenge any reduction of Christianity to any form of ethnic self-congratulations. They demand Christian self-and-group-transcendence of the ambiguities present in *any* particular cultural expression.

Second, the universal-particular or public-private problematic of Christian theology is too often formulated without an adequate consideration of the full alternatives. In fact, the emergence of "ethnic theologies" (such as black theology or Italian-American theology) is not a plea for particularism or private language. Indeed ethnic theology can occasion further reflections upon the fuller meanings of public language itself. As a single example of that fuller meaning, one may reflect upon the phenomenon of the "classic." Intuitively we all recognize that the great classics of our heritage, including our religious heritage, are both deeply particular in origin and expression, yet genuinely public in disclosive and transformative power. Indeed, any classic involves a significant paradox: precisely an artist's or thinker's fidelity to his/her own concrete and particular personal, social, cultural, and religious heritage occasions the emergence of a public form of discourse. Any classic, however particular its origins and form, bears publicly disclosive and transformative power for all human beings. When Thomas Mann attempted to write a "universal" novel he produced *Joseph and His Brothers*—a work best described as a novelistic period-piece. When Mann explored his own German heritage at depth he produced a novel like *Doctor Faustus*—a work widely acknowledged as a modern classic, as disclosive of human possibility and limitation to all persons. One need not personally experience the intense conflicts peculiar to some Irish-American family structures in order to find Eugene O'Neill's classic drama *Long Day's Journey Into Night* publicly disclosive. One need not be Italian to appreciate the haunting disclosiveness of Federico Fellini's films, nor be Italian-American to find that Martin Scorsese's films speak to one's own experience of profound human limitation.

To encourage ethnic theologies, therefore, is not to endorse a retreat into "private" languages. Rather, ethnic theologies should encourage the emergence of contemporary Christian theological classics. Any good ethnic theologian's fidelity to a particular cultural apprehension of religious values should prove both disclosive and transformative—in a word, "public"—for us all. As public, ethnic theologies should encourage that fidelity to concrete experience which is a hallmark of all good contemporary theology. As particular, they may also aid that enrichment of human possibility which the emergence of theological pluralism fosters. This affirmation of pluralism in theology leads to reflection upon the implications of ethnicity for a theology of pluralism.

III. THEOLOGY, ETHNICITY AND PLURALISM

Thesis: Ethnicity may help theologians to negate the imposition of univocal cultural visions and to rearticulate the classical theological tradition of analogy in an explicitly pluralistic fashion.

The heart of the recent revival of ethnic self-consciousness in the American Catholic context is the call for cultural justice from society and from church. Like most prophetic calls for justice, the ethnic demand takes an initial tone of negation. The famous "melting-pot" theory of America has been clearly, forcefully, and justly negated: first by American blacks and more recently by several other ethnic groups. Why, in the name of American and Christian ideals and principles of justice, should any American black, native American, Slovak-American, or Italian-American be told, in effect, that he must abandon his own cultural apprehension of values and become an Anglo-Saxon in order to be an "American"? If the "melting-pot" theory of America ever made sense (a dubious proposition), it surely makes no sense now.

In an analogous manner, within the church any imposition of a pre-Vatican II, neo-Scholastic, "Roman School" theology upon all Catholics is an affront to the Catholic sense of justice.[4] Neither the American ideals embodied in the American constitution and institutions, nor the Catholic ideals of social justice—now applied to the cultural realm—can in principle countenance such cultural imposition. That a central religious and theological common identity should exist for Roman Catholic Christians remains a sound theological position. That a common *polity* is needed for the United States and even that there is a common *cultural* American apprehension of values (as signalized in the "American civil religion" debate) also seems a sound principle and an empirical fact. Yet these truisms must not become the occasion to impose a single Anglo-Saxon cultural apprehension of values upon all Americans. In the church this same principle disallows the imposition of a culturally neo-scholastic theology upon all Catholics.

To negate univocal cultural visions in both society and church is also to affirm the basic enrichment which cultural diversity can bring to church and society. Yet one need not rest content in mere negations, nor even in an all too-easy "let a thousand flowers bloom" approach to societal and theological pluralism. Instead a theologian may appeal to a once familiar theologoumenon: the theological language of analogy. Analogy, as is well known, was developed by theologians as a "middle" language used to avoid the extremes of equivocity (in this context, the assertion of an unreflective pluralism comprised of unrelated and exclusive cultural particularisms), and univocity (in this context, the imposition of *one* cultural apprehension of values upon all alternatives). As the earlier discussion of the classic indicates, a key to the present question of pluralism may well lie in learning anew the skills of the classical Catholic analogical vision of reality. For the genuinely analogical mind, precisely by its responsible commitment to its own cultural apprehension of values, is freed to understand others. Analogy enables each participant to listen to, learn from, and eventually even partly appropriate alternative cultural visions of human value and possibility into her/his own horizon. The analogical mind learns to develop analogies which allow one to differentiate, to appropriate, and eventually to integrate a different vision of reality from one's own. As an entire community learns these analogical skills, ethnic pluralism—including its theological expressions—becomes not a threat but a promise: a promise of an enriched cultural self-understanding for all persons; a promise to develop a community-wide analogical vision embracing the diversity of several cultural heritages.

IV. ETHNIC THEOLOGY AND THE SEARCH FOR CULTURALLY TRANSCENDENT CHRISTIAN PRINCIPLES

Thesis: Every ethnic theology needs to articulate culturally transcendent Christian principles relevant to the particular problems of that culture.

Every particular form of theology bears its own possibilities and its own peculiar temptations. For example, any theologian uninterested in the experiential roots of his/her own cultural form of theology may produce helpful general principles but is ordinarily unequipped to provide more specific guidance. Alternatively, any ethnic theology which explicitly relates itself to a particular cultural heritage will prove invaluable for illuminating the positive theological meaning of "experience" and "pluralism." The peculiar temptation of any theology of experience and pluralism, however, should also be noted: the temptation to ignore Christianity's transformative demands upon any cultural heritage.[5]

One need not be Barthian to assume that central Christian theological conviction. Indeed the Barthian model for the relationship between Christianity and culture (basically a confrontation model) is now widely and justly considered theologically inadequate. Yet the direct contrary of the Barthian confrontation model, the "liberal" identity model, is even more inappropriate. Surely Karl Barth's profound theological convictions, articulated in the Barmen Declaration of the Confessing Church remains a gripping, indeed classic, statement of Christianity in the modern period. Barth's hermeneutics of suspicion upon all forms of cultural Christianity, in his test case, the all-too-"ethnic" "German Christians," remains sound.

In sum, Christianity must continue to articulate culturally transcendent principles challenging any cultural expression of religion (including Christendom). In extreme situations, as in Nazi Germany, Christianity must confront the demonic distortions of a particular cultural heritage with its witness to Jesus Christ. All ethnic theologies, therefore, should attempt to articulate not only disclosive possibilities for "experience" and "pluralism." They should also strive to articulate theologically transformative, explicitly Christian demands and possibilities for the cultural situation.

In the Catholic tradition, the understanding of relationship between Christianity and culture is ordinarily neither a liberal "identity model" nor a neo-orthodox "confrontation model," but rather a specifically Catholic "transformation model." For example, a transformation model is clearly implied by such central Catholic theological positions as the Catholic understanding of the relationship between faith and reason or of grace and nature. As a specific example of such culturally transcendent principles in the Catholic tradition, one may turn to the Catholic understandings of love and justice as the latter are expressed through particular ethnic traditions.

Love, for the Catholic Christian, is best understood as the theological virtue of charity whereby the utterly gratuitous gift of divine *agape* in Jesus Christ transforms, but does not destroy, the endless strivings of human *eros*. Catholic *caritas*, moreover, in terms of its demands for human relationships, has as its distinctive characteristic an *equal* concern for *each* concrete neighbor. In its more developed state, Catholic charity ordinarily involves two further characteristics: the heedlessness of self-sacrificial love and the redemptive possibilities of suffering love.[6]

With this theological understanding of Christian love, one may turn to certain ethnic cultural expressions of "charity" to see how *caritas* may function as culturally transcendent and transformative. An oft-cited ethnic difference between "northern" and "southern" European peoples (and their American counterparts) is the character and role of expressiveness in the experience of suffering. As far as I can see, there is nothing in the theological tradition to challenge either the expansive expressiveness of the southern "Italian" response to bereavement or the more inhibited attitude of the Anglo-Saxon peoples. In short, either "outward" expression may indicate a truly Christian inner attitude of a loving, as pained but accepting, response to the intense suffering of personal bereavement. The issue between these differences of expression, therefore, is strictly cultural: the religiously transformative principle of charity as suffering love may be present or absent in either.

On the other hand, even that highest form of Christian charity, self-sacrificial love, can receive ethnic distortion. For example, in Irish-American culture (which is my own principal and valued ethnic heritage) "self-sacrifice" can sometimes become a "code word" which imposes certain "convenient," even selfish desires of a particular "extended family" upon

some member of the family, often an elder daughter. Yet even if one grants
(as I do) that Christian self-sacrificial love may involve a heedless abandonment of one's own desires for authentic self-fulfillment and one's own plan of
life, strictly theological suspicions should remain upon all such ethnically
determined expressions. For the culturally transcendent Christian principle of
transformative, self-sacrificial love may not be reduced to the ambiguities,
much less the various demonic distortions, of any particular ethnic heritage.

In the Catholic theological tradition, moreover, not only "faith" and
"love" but also "reason" and "justice" are affirmed as possessing culturally
transcendent possibilities. The Catholic theological commitment to meta-
physical or transcendental reflection in theology is the most obvious example
of this affirmation. Still, the same belief is clearly present in the Catholic
tradition of social justice. In American pluralistic society, for example, a
Catholic theologian believes that, in principle, the cause of ethnic cultural
justice can be won in that public forum comprised of "all reasonable persons
of good will." In that same situation, a Catholic theologian can, in principle,
enter into discussions of social polity issues on the same assumption of the
culturally transcending possibilities of reasoned discourse affirmed by such
secular theorists as John Rawls in *A Theory of Justice*. Before various "full
theories of the social good" are advanced (to use the Rawlsian vocabulary),
all parties to the discussion can agree in principle upon commonly acceptable
principles of justice. This theological commitment to the self-transcendent
and group-transcendent possibilities of authentic "reason" and public
discourse is a crucial resource of the Catholic heritage. One cannot but hope
that the healthy resurgence of interest in ethnic theologies among American
Catholics will not become the occasion to bypass the Catholic tradition's
consistent belief in the possibilities of *common* reasoned discourse on
questions of justice for society.

This hope becomes particularly urgent when one moves, as one must, past
the discussion of "cultural justice" issues in the realm of culture into "social
justice" issues in the realm of polity. For example, the issues of "neighborhood" and "parish," so correctly emphasized by recent American Catholic
ethnic thinkers as too long ignored primary social realities in our society and
church, involve issues of justice in the realms of both culture and polity. To
conflate those issues into a single one is to refuse justice to the complexity of
the several justice issues involved in the two realms, much less to the intricate
relationships between the realms. As a single example of the complexity of
social polity justice issues in the American setting, consider the following
familiar example: When one compares the social injustice inflicted upon the
native American and the black in American society to the social injustice
endured by later ethnic groups, one cannot but affirm a difference more of
kind than of degree: as one commentator has observed, it is like the
difference between a broken back and a broken arm. Such qualitative

differences should not become occasions to ignore the injustice still suffered by ethnic persons and neighborhoods in the United States, yet surely must remain relevant to any community-wide discussion of social polity issues.

If the resurgence of interest in ethnicity among theologians becomes an occasion for theological enrichment in the church and aids the struggle for cultural justice in society, then the yet more complex issues of social polity can be informed, and perhaps even transformed, by a reinvigorated public discourse in which Christian theology will play a partial but vital role.

Notes

1. This clear definition is that employed by The Center for the Study of American Pluralism at The University of Chicago. For an example of the use of this definition, cf. Andrew M. Greeley, *The Communal Catholic* (New York: Seabury, 1976), pp. 127-51. For representative articles by American Catholics (including Geno Baroni, Michael Novak, and Virgil Elizondo), cf. the "Ethnicity in the Church" issue of the *New Catholic World* (May/June, 1976), pp. 101-43.

2. This definition may be found in Daniel Bell, *The Cultural Contradictions of Capitalism* (New York: Basic, 1976), pp. 10-12. I have modified Professor Bell's definition of the realm of "culture" in accordance with the studies of Clifford Geertz in *The Interpretation of Cultures* (New York: Basic, 1973), esp. pp. 3-33, 87-126, and in relationship to my own work on symbol in theology.

3. For the arguments for this definition, cf. my *Blessed Rage for Order: The New Pluralism in Theology* (New York: Seabury, 1975).

4. To negate the univocal imposition of either Anglo-Saxon culture upon all Americans or neo-Scholastic theology upon all Catholics is not, of course, to negate the extraordinary richness of Anglo-American cultures or the real contributions to theology of the neo-Scholastics.

5. For a still classic study of these realities cf. H. Richard Niebuhr, *Christ and Culture* (New York: Harper, 1960). I plan to expand upon the meaning and defense of my own systematic categories employed in this work—especially "classic," "analogy," "disclosure" and "transformation" models—in a forthcoming (1977) book entitled *The Analogical Imagination in Theology*.

6. For a clear discussion of these issues, cf. Gene Outka, *Agape: An Ethical Analysis* (New Haven: Yale University Press, 1974).

Gregory Baum

Editorial Summary

CHRISTIANS living in a troubled world look to scripture and tradition for light and inspiration. Since ethnicity has emerged in many parts of the world as an important issue and since grave injustices have been inflicted on people because national governments have been unable to protect the plural ethnic heritage of the population, ethnic pluralism has become a major ethico-political problem. It could even be said that the political tradition of the West, and of the world in general, has so little wisdom in regard to ethnic pluralism and the protection of particular traditions that the major crimes of the last decades have been the oppression of minorities. We have witnessed genocides; we have seen the legal oppression of minorities; we recognize the discrimination inflicted on ethnic communities. This issue of *Concilium* deals with one aspect of this problem: the emergence of ethnicity. At this time, almost every country has to deal with the ethnic issue in one way or another. What does Christian theology have to say to this ethico-political problem?

While we turn to the scriptures for wisdom, we do not expect to find in them the specific answers to the questions posed by contemporary political life. Still, according to the preceding articles on peoplehood and plurality in the scriptures, the Bible offers the powerful double message that God is at one and the same time the lover of humanity and the lover of a particular people. The Bible affirms both universality and particularity. God is inseparably the creator of pluriformity and the author of unity. This double message of the Bible reminds the church of that aspect of social life that is being forgotten or suppressed in the world to which it belongs. At times when a single race, people or tribe affirms itself as superior to others and adopts an aggressive stance toward humanity (we all remember such cases in recent history) the biblical message summons Christians to defend the unity of humankind as a family of brothers and sisters, but at times when particular races, peoples, or ethnic groups discover themselves as oppressed, the same scriptures call the church to a new appreciation of pluriformity and the defense of particular traditions.

While the Bible defines the horizon in which Christians want to reflect on the problems raised by ethnicity, it is far too early to construct a theology of ethnicity. The two exploratory articles, by John Shea and David Tracy, refer to the American experience alone. And even here, as David Tracy clearly states, it has been necessary in a preliminary exploration to bracket from consideration the oppression due to race, class and gender. Since in actual fact the emergence of ethnic self-awareness in America takes place within a complex political and economic situation, one may wonder how far it is possible to separate the notion of ethnicity from power. Still, theologians must make a beginning. The great difficulty of reflecting on ethnicity from a theological point of view is that social scientists have not come to an agreement on the meaning and social function of ethnicity in various parts of the world. The pluralism of settler countries, such as the U.S.A., Canada and Australia, which have been created as colonies and populated by immigrants from developed cultures, is quite different from the pluralism of traditional European countries, in which people have slowly developed from tribal existence to modern civilization. Settler countries have usually suppressed a native population; they have continued to attract immigrants from Europe and other parts, and in many instances forced some peoples, through slave trade or political annexation, to live within their frontiers. Thus in the U.S.A. neither the native Indians nor the black people nor the Mexican-Americans and Puerto Ricans are derived from immigrant stock. Should they be classified as ethnic communities? Most sociologists consider ethnic groups only those communities that have been derived from immigrants, mainly European, and do not belong to the founding nation. In Canada, neither the French nor the British regard themselves as ethnics. According to this usage, the sociological definition of ethnicity is related to power.

Social thinkers do not agree on the meaning and social function of ethnicity in North America. Since the new stress on ethnic self-understanding occurred after the black power movement, it is not always clear whether the new black self-affirmation has stimulated other particular communities in America to affirm their self-worth and their difference, or whether the new stress on ethnicity is an attempt of Americans of European stock to relativize the complaints of the blacks. In Canada, the stress on multi-culturalism is certainly a political policy that wants to relativize the French fact and weaken the original bi-national character of the Canadian union.

Social thinkers are divided on the social function of ethnic consciousness in America. Some stress the positive side. The expanded ethnic self-understanding, they show, provides people in modern, industrial society with a new sense of belonging; it assures the survival of communal values in an individualistic society; it creates cohesion and solidarity in neighborhoods and thus protects the modern city from decay; it expresses the desire for decentralization at a time when more and more power passes into the hands of the government; it brings people in touch with their historical roots and gives them access to creativity, of which mass society has deprived them.

Other social thinkers are more sensitive to the negative aspects. They claim that most immigrant groups have brought with them a culture and a language that bear the marks of the oppression under which they lived in the old world, and that to stress ethnic self-identity, unaccompanied by educational opportunities, makes these people sentimentally attached to an impoverished and inarticulate past and prevents them from developing with the cultural movements of their new home. It is true, for instance, that German and Polish Catholics arriving in Canada after World War II often refuse to join the older German and Polish parishes because they seem quaint to them, remnants of a previous century; even the language used there is often reduced to the simplest sentence structures and thus ceases to be an adequate tool for talking about the basic political realities of the country. Other social thinkers hold that the new stress on ethnicity weakens working class solidarity and hence has important political implications. If a Portuguese worker in Canada is a Portuguese before he is a worker, then his primary solidarity will be with his ethnic community and not with the working class; and since in Canada labor is identified with a political party, this would affect his voting. The social function of ethnicity may well differ from country to country.

Seeing that social thinkers are divided in their evaluation of the emergence of ethnicity, it is difficult for theologians to engage in theological reflection on it unless they are willing to study the various sociological and political analyses and decide for themselves which of these are the most convincing. Since the Catholic Church within its own ecclesiastical tradition often pays insufficient attention to ethnic pluralism, this is an urgent topic. It is the hope of the editors that this issue of *Concilium* will stimulate theologians to engage in new research.

Contributors

WALKER CONNOR, professor of political science and faculty exchange scholar at the State University of New York (Brockport) is currently a fellow at the Woodrow Wilson International Center for Scholars, Washington, D.C. He has published numerous articles on ethnic nationalism as a global phenomenon.

MARY CONNOR has been a long-time research associate and collaborator of Walker Connor in the study of nationalism.

MARIA BORRIS, economist and sociologist, conducts research and studies for public and private clients in the areas of general, educational, and industrial sociology. She also teaches in the Academy of Work at the University of Frankfurt am Main. Among her published works are *Die Benachteiligung der Mädchen in den Schulen der BRD* ([4] 1975) and *Ausländische Arbeiter in einer Grosstadt: Eine empirische Untersuchung am Beispiel Frankfurt* ([3] 1976).

JOHN SIMPSON, an ordained minister of the United Presbyterian Church in the United States of America, is assistant professor of sociology at Erindale College, University of Toronto. Among his publications in the sociology of religion are "Presbyterian Laymen and the Confession of 1967: A Case Study in Status Politics," *The Christian Ministry* 1 (1970), and "The Precarious Enterprise of Ministry," *Pastoral Psychology* 25 (1976).

MICHEL DE VERTEUIL (educated at University College, Dublin, and at the University of Fribourg), HENRY CHARLES (educated at University College, Dublin, and at the Gregorian University, Rome), and CLYDE HARVEY (educated at the University of the West Indies and at Louvain University, Belgium) are Roman Catholic priests, affiliated with the Seminary of St. John Vianney, Tunapuna, Trinidad.

EWA MORAWSKA, born and educated in Poland, received her Ph.D. in sociology from Boston University. She is presently working in the Immigration Research Institute of the Polish Academy of Sciences in Poznan. Among her publications are "The Theme of 'Native' vs. 'Alien' in the Writings of the Polish Emigration in France, 1832-1846," ZNAK (1973), and (with Irwin T. Sanders) "Polish-American Community Life: A Survey of Research," Community Sociological Monograph Series, vol. 2, Boston University.

MARY DURKIN is a visiting faculty member at the School for New Learning of DePaul University, Chicago. She is a theological consultant to the National Center for Urban Ethnic Affairs and a member of the board of directors of the Catholic Conference on Ethnic and Neighborhood Affairs. She is the author of *The Suburban Woman: Her Changing Role in the Church* (1975).

RAYMOND BRETON is currently a professor of sociology at the University of Toronto. His professional concerns and publications have focused upon immigrants, industrial workers, nationalism in Quebec, inter-ethnic attitudes, ethnic diversity, and urban ethnic pluralism.

ROGELIO DUOCASTELLA ROSELL was the founder and, from 1957 to 1963, director of Caritas's Centro de Estudios de Sociologia Aplicada (CESA), and editor of *Documentation Social*. In 1963 he created the Instituto de Sociologia y Psicologia Alicada (ISPA), where he has undertaken more than a hundred studies, and whose Escuela de Formacion de Investigadores Sociales was opened in 1972.

ANDREW M. GREELEY is director of the Center for the Study of American Pluralism at the National Opinion Research Center of the University of Chicago. Among his most recent books are *Catholic Schools in a Declining Church; The Communal Catholic; The Great Mysteries; Ethnicity, Denomination and Inequality*; and, forthcoming, *American Catholics: A Social Portrait* and *The Mary Myth*.

BERNHARD ANDERSON, an ordained minister of the United Methodist Church, is professor of Old Testament theology at Princeton Theological Seminary. Previously he was dean of the Theological School and professor of biblical theology at Drew University, Madison, New Jersey. With the late G. Ernest Wright he cooperated in launching archaeological excavation at the site of biblical Shechem. Among his books are *Understanding the Old Testament* (³ 1975), *Creation versus Chaos* (1967), and *Out of the Depths: The Psalms Speak for Us Today* (1970, 1974).

ROLAND MURPHY, O. Carm., is professor of Old Testament studies at the

Duke University Divinity School in Durham, North Carolina. A member of the editorial board of *Concilium*, he is the author of several articles and books dealing with the Old Testament.

BRUCE VAWTER, C.M., is professor and president of the Department of Theology at DePaul University, Chicago. Among his published works are *A Path through Genesis, The Bible in the Church, The Conscience of Israel, New Paths through the Bible*, and *Biblical Inspiration*.

JOHN SHEA teaches theology at St. Mary of the Lake Seminary, Mundelein, Illinois. He is the author of three books—*What a Modern Catholic Believes about Sin, What a Modern Catholic Believes about Heaven and Hell*, and *The Challenge of Jesus*—and of numerous articles in *Chicago Studies, The Ecumenist*, and the *Notre Dame Journal of Education*.

DAVID TRACY is professor of philosophical theology at the Divinity School of the University of Chicago. He is the author of *The Achievement of Bernard Lonergan* (1970) and *Blessed Rage for Order: The New Pluralism in Theology* (1975). He contributes to several reviews and is an editor of the *Journal of Religion* and the *Journal of the American Academy of Religion*.

GREGORY BAUM is professor of theology and sociology at St. Michael's College of the University of Toronto. He is editor of *The Ecumenist* and the *Journal of Ecumenical Studies*, and author of *Man Becoming* (1970), *New Horizon* (1972), and *Religion and Alienation* (1975).